THE BAPTISTS:

THEIR

ORIGIN, CONTINUITY, PRINCIPLES, SPIRIT, POLITY,
POSITION, AND INFLUENCE.

A VINDICATION.

BY

T. G. JONES, D.D.

Philadelphia:
AMERICAN BAPTIST PUBLICATION SOCIETY,
530 ARCH STREET.

CONTENTS.

THE BAPTISTS.

I.

PRELIMINARY STATEMENTS.

True Christianity always opposed—Opposition to Christ himself—To his faithful followers in every age—To the Baptists especially—The opposition undeserved—Testimony of others—Real cause of the hostility—It still continues—Is softened but not subdued—Shows itself in unjust imputations—Proposed Vindication.

WHATEVER its outward forms or modes of expression, genuine Christianity has always been opposed. Having all the offense of the cross, it meets in every carnal mind a foe. Its Divine Author himself encountered the most constant and unrelenting opposition. In the annals of the world there is no instance of so causeless, and malignant, and perpetual a persecution as that which the Lord of Life and Glory suffered. It commenced with the beginning of his public ministry, and continued till its sublimely tragic close. The very embodiment of truth, men called him an impostor. The truest friend of the people, they charged him with betraying them. The most peaceful and law-abiding of all earth's citizens, they said he sowed the seeds of sedition, and plotted against the government: The most unworldly and unselfish, the meekest and lowliest of beings, they charged him with seeking human honor and an earthly crown. Recoiling with infinite revulsion from the least irreverence, they sought to fix upon him the guilt of blasphemy. Performing miracles the most stupendous and sublime, as well as the most beneficent, they pronounced them the work, not of celestial, but infernal power. When he gave to the suffering and weary body, and the yet more suffering and weary soul, rest on the Sabbath, they charged him with desecration of the holy day. Whithersoever he went they followed him, and beset his path, seeking to "entangle him in his talk"—to involve him in contradictions and false issues, and thus to make him, by some unguarded word, odious to the people or obnoxious to the government. Having at length, through the bribery of a false friend, compassed his betrayal, they condemned him to death, and delivered him to the Gentiles to mock and to scourge, and to crucify him. And even when he lay still and stiff in death, their hate knew no relentings

They spoke of him with cold contempt, and bitter malignity, as "that deceiver."

Nor was it long after the consummation of the wicked but futile measures of his enemies upon his sacred person, before his followers all realized the truth of his declaration, "If they have persecuted me, they will also persecute you." They were "every where spoken against." They were reviled, persecuted, defamed, accounted as the filth of the world, and the offscouring of all things. Their chief teachers were seized, bound, thrust into prison, and some of them inhumanly murdered.

And as the weary years rolled on, the opposition they encountered knew no abatement. They were cast into noisome dungeons, thrown to wild beasts, burned at the stake, and tormented in every way which the ingenuity of men, aided and inspired by the rage of hell, could invent. Their very women suffered the most shameful indignities, and the most cruel tortures. The more they resembled Christ, the more they breathed his spirit, the more closely they followed in his footsteps, the more obnoxious were they to their persecutors.

In later times, still contending earnestly for the faith once delivered to the saints, they were opposed with equal persistency and rage, and myriads sealed with their blood their testimony to the truth. Even the greater light and increasing liberty of modern ages, were slow to bring them relief. They taught the purest and holiest truths, they lived the purest and holiest lives, yet still were they constantly and cruelly opposed. Their doctrines were grossly misrepresented. Their own character was vilely slandered. They were deprived of their natural and social, civil and religious rights. They were arrested upon false charges, carried through the processes of mock trials, and summarily condemned to the most cruel and ignominious punishments. Thus perished thousands and hundreds of thousands of faithful witnesses for God. The spirit of their persecutors often seemed more diabolic than human. It was so calmly and coldly cruel. It so delighted in tears and blood, in sighs and shrieks, in despair and death. It had no pity. It knew no relentings. It could be moved by no pleading look of truth and purity, of helplessness and innocence. It was as hard and unyielding to feminine gentleness and sweetness, youthful simplicity and beauty, as to stern and rugged manhood, duplicity and ugliness. So ingenious, so hypocritical, it could have been inspired only by the subtlety of the serpent, and the deep deception of the father of lies. Others have their hates—but they seem human hates. The hates of these so-called religious persecutors seemed the very hates of hell.

But of all the followers of Jesus, none have so constantly and so deeply suffered as the Baptists. "It is difficult," says Benedict, "to find language to describe the disposition which for ages was shown towards the old Waldenses, Anabaptists, and all kindred communities, under whatever names they passed, who were made to suffer and feel the rigor of the laws which were continually enacted against them by all classes of rulers, civil and ecclesiastical. The concentrated rays of their scorching indignation with focal intensity were made to fall on a defenseless people, who had neither the means nor the disposition to defend themselves. The full vials of their wrath, with awful regurgitations, were poured out upon their devoted heads. Century after century the Christian world, so-called, was mad against them. Catholics and Protestants went hand in hand in their efforts to protect the infant system, and by fire and sword to drive every vestige of anti-pedobaptism from the earth."

Persecuted in one country they fled into another. But, alas! no country afforded them a refuge. Driven from the Continent, they fled to England. Driven from England, they fled beyond seas to Massachusetts. Driven from Massachusetts, they fled, as of old, to "the wilderness," where alone they found an asylum.

Now, why this universal and unrelenting opposition? They surely did not deserve it. "They stood alone," says Underhill, referring to the Bap

History of the Baptists, p. 932.

tists of the early part of the seventeenth century, "amidst all their cotemporaries for liberal and enlightened views. Calumny, contumely, reproach, and persecution, failed to turn them from their high and holy calling. Freedom to worship God, as each for himself thought right, even when others might think it heresy, they nobly struggled for to the end. They were the first to pioneer the way through the forests of human superstition, the morasses of human inventions, and the barriers of human usurpations. A forlorn hope, they assailed the huge fortress of human tyranny. But *God was their refuge and their strength.* They made the costly outlay for that inheritance, whose rich and pleasant fruit we daily gather." Another eminent member of their communion, Dr. Wayland, in a recent work upon their Principles and Practices, referring to them generally, says,—"Our whole history is in the highest degree honorable to us as a Christian sect. If any sect has occasion to glory, we more. If any man among us does not feel a manly pride in the sentiments which have distinguished us, and in the manner in which we have maintained them, there must exist something peculiar, either in his head or his heart."

From others, too, comes testimony in their behalf of the highest value. "Many of the first set-

Rel. Lib. p. 215.

tlers in Massachusetts were Baptists," says Cotton Mather, a zealous opponent of them, "and as holy, and watchful, and fruitful, and heavenly a people, as perhaps any in the world." The celebrated John Locke, in his Essay on Toleration, says that the Baptists were the first and only propounders of "absolute liberty, just and true liberty, equal and impartial liberty." Dr. Chalmers says, "Let it never be forgotten of the Particular Baptists of England, that they form the denomination of Fuller, and Carey, and Ryland, and Hall, and Foster: that they have originated among the greatest of all missionary enterprises; that they have enriched the Christian literature of our country with authorship of the most exalted piety, as well as of the first talent, and the first eloquence; that they have waged a very noble and successful war with the hydra of antinomianism; that perhaps there is not a more intellectual community of ministers in our island, or who have put forth, to their number, a greater amount of mental power, and mental activity in the defense and illustration of our common faith; and, what is still better than all the triumphs of genius or understanding, who, by their zeal and fidelity, and pastoral labor among the congregations which they have reared, have done more to swell the lists of genuine discipleship in the walks of private society, and thus both to uphold and extend the living Christianity of our nation." Bancroft, the historian, in his account of the Baptist colony of Rhode Island, says, "Freedom of conscience, unlimited freedom of mind, was, from the first, the trophy of the Baptists."[1] Speaking of the Baptists of Germany, he thus strongly and eloquently expresses himself,—"With greater consistency than Luther, they applied the doctrines of the Reformation to the social positions of life, and threatened an end to priest-craft, and king-craft, spiritual domination, tithes, and vassalage. The party was trodden under foot with foul reproaches, and most arrogant scorn, and its history is written in the blood of myriads of the German peasantry; but its principles, secure in their immortality, escaped with Roger Williams to Providence; and his colony is the witness that naturally the paths of the Baptists are paths of freedom, of pleasantness, and peace."[2]

Dr. Price, in his History of Nonconformity, speaking of the Baptists, says, "It belonged to the members of a calumniated and despised sect, few in numbers and poor in circumstances, to bring forth to public view, in their simplicity and omnipotence, those immortal principles which are now universally recognized as of Divine authority and of universal obligation. Other writers of more distinguished name succeeded, and robbed them of their honor; but their title is so good, and the amount of ser-

[1] Hist. U. S. vol. ii. p. p. 66-67 [2] Hist. U. S. vol. ii. p. 459.

vice they performed on behalf of the common interests of humanity is so incalculable, that an impartial posterity must assign to them their due meed of praise." Even the Romanist Cardinal Hosius, referring to the Baptists before and at the time of the Reformation, pays them this high tribute: "If you behold their cheerfulness in suffering persecutions, the Anabaptists run before all other heretics. If you will have regard to the number, it is like that in multitude they would swarm above all others, if they were not grievously plagued and cut off with the knife of persecution. If you have an eye to the outward appearance of godliness, both the Lutherans and Zuinglians must needs grant that they far pass them. If you will be moved by the boasting of the word of God, these be no less bold than Calvin to preach, and their doctrine must stand aloft above all the glory of the world, must stand invincible above all power, because it is not their word, but the word of the living God. Neither do they cry less boldly than Luther, that with their doctrine, which is the word of God, they shall judge the angels. And surely, how many soever have written against this heresy, whether they were Catholics or heretics, [Reformers,] they were able to overthrow it, not so much by the testimony of the Scriptures, as by the authority of the church."[1]

1 Hatchet of Heresies translated by R. Shacklock, fol. 48, edit. 1565. Underhill, pp. 88-89.

Why then, we again ask, the constant and bitter opposition to the Baptists? That distinguished English Baptist already quoted, Underhill, thus indicates the source of much of it: "We have, however, discovered the real cause of the unanimous hostility these despised people encountered. Papist and Protestant, Puritan and Brownist, with one consent, laid aside their differences, to condemn and punish a sect, a heresy, an opinion, which threw prostrate their favorite church, their politico-ecclesiastical power, their extravagant assumptions, and their unscriptural theories. The Papists abhorred them: for if this heresy prevailed, a church hoary with age, laden with the spoils of many lands, rich in the merchandise of souls, must be utterly broken and destroyed. The Protestants hated them: for their cherished headship, their worldly alliances, the pomps and circumstances of a state religion, must be debased before the kingly crown of Jesus. The Puritans defamed them: for Baptist sentiments were too liberal and free for those who sought a papal authority over conscience, and desired the sword of the higher powers to enforce their 'holy discipline' on an unconverted people. The Brownists avoided them: for their principle of liberty was too broad, and to this they added the crime of rejecting the Lord's little ones from the fold."[1]

[1] Rel. Lib. p. 200, 201.

But whatever may have been the cause or causes of it, the fact that these people have, in all ages, encountered the most strenuous opposition is clear. That this opposition continues, to a very considerable extent, is equally clear. The ancient opponents of the Baptists cast out their name as evil. They had no proper means of defense before human tribunals. Their voices were silenced—their books were burned, and themselves driven out into the wilderness, and into the dens and caves of the earth. Their only proper record was on high. Tradition, many-tongued and false, slandered them. The muse of history, whose boast is truth, deceived and led astray, slandered them. These slanders, imbedded in the strata of history, have continued, miserable fossils, until this day. And hence much of the *odium theologicum* of the past, clings tenaciously to the Baptists still.

Although in our own land, especially, they now suffer no fines, nor imprisonments, no civil disabilities whatever, they yet have great reason to complain of the injustice still done them. The opposition is softened, but it is not subdued. In the social circle, through the press, and even in the pulpit, they are often severely assailed. Imputations the most unjust and injurious are constantly made against them.

For this injustice, the Baptists are compelled to arraign the candor and intelligence, or the Christian courtesy and kindness, of their opponents. It pains them to be under the necessity of doing either. But there seems to them no alternative. Those who so persistently oppose them, are, without doubt, grossly ignorant of their true character and history, their real principles and spirit, or they are swayed by prejudices and passions the most unreasonable and unworthy. In either case we submit that the latter have as little reason for self-complacency as the former for self-abasement.

Some of the opponents of the Baptists *openly* and *boldly* bring accusations against them. Others, with *an air of charitable indifference*, simply *suggest* them. With *softened, subdued utterance,* they disparage

> "With faint praise, assent with civil leer
> And without sneering, teach the rest to sneer
> Willing to wound, and yet afraid to strike,
> Just hint a fault and hesitate dislike."

In the following pages we shall attempt a brief vindication of the Baptists from some of these bold charges, and covert insinuations. Those which we propose to notice, may all, perhaps, be properly regarded as having reference to the ORIGIN, CONTINUITY, PRINCIPLES, SPIRIT, POLITY, and GENERAL INFLUENCE UPON THE WORLD, of the Baptists. And under these heads we propose to consider them.

II.

ORIGIN OF THE BAPTISTS.

Late Origin alleged against the Baptists—Universal belief among Baptists respecting their Origin—Weight as an argument of this belief—Apostolic origin of the Baptists—Scriptural evidence—Analysis of the Commission—Procedure of the Apostles—Constituents of the First Churches—Leading characteristics—Substantially identical with those of modern Baptists—No necessity for tracing Unbroken Succession.

IT is often objected to the Baptists that while they claim to be more strictly than others, the true churches of Christ, they actually had no existence until many centuries after the first promulgation and establishment of the gospel. Many of their opponents confidently affirm that they originated in Germany, and so late as the sixteenth century. Even so respectable a person as the Rev. Albert Barnes, of Philadelphia, author of popular commentaries upon the Scriptures, not long since said of the Baptists that "as a denomination they are but of yesterday"—and that "they have not as a foundation for their exclusiveness, even the poor pretension of the Episcopalians, that they can trace their history back to the apostolic times; for there were times, and those not far remote in the history of the world, when the Baptist denomination was not. For more than three-fourths of the history of the church on the earth, Christianity has made its way somehow among the nations—converting sinners, overthrowing idolatry, diffusing knowledge, establishing colleges and schools, comforting the afflicted, and sustaining the dying, *without* the Baptist idea that men must be immersed—and that the blessings of the covenant descend only on those whose children are not baptized." To the same purport wrote Dr. Miller, of Princeton, some years since, in his work on Infant Baptism. And the well-known Dr. Nevin, in 1852, in the Mercersburg Review, after pronouncing the faith of the Baptists a "new faith"—and their system a "modern system," a "thing comparatively of yesterday," "nothing more in fact than the last phase of what is called Orthodox Puritanism," proceeds thus to apostrophize the new scheme: "Who art thou, upstart system! that thou shouldest set thyself in such proud style above the universal church of antiquity—the immediate successors of the apostles, the noble army of martyrs, the goodly fellowship of the fathers, the vast cloud of witnesses that look down upon us from those ages of faith—charging it with wholesale superstition and folly, and requiring us to renounce its creed, the whole scheme and habit of its religious life, and to accept from thy hands, in place of it, another form of belief, another scheme of doctrine altogether, as infallibly true and right? Who gave thee this authority? Whence came such infallibility?" In similar strains, do many others, of less note, also express themselves.

That these views of their origin and character are both uncharitable and unjust, the Baptists universally believe. They have always maintained that their churches are as ancient as Christianity itself. That their foundations were laid by no less honorable hands than those of Christ and his apostles. In all ages since the first, the Baptists have believed their denomination more ancient than themselves. The American Baptists deny that they owe their origin to Roger Williams. The English Baptists will not grant that John Smyth or Thomas Helwysse was their founder. The Welsh Baptists strenuously contend that they received their creed in the first century, from those who had obtained it, direct, from the apostles themselves. The Dutch Baptists trace their spiritual pedigree up to the same source. The German Baptists maintained that they were older than the Reformation, older than the corrupt hierarchy which it sought to reform. The Waldensian Baptists boasted an ancestry far older than Waldo, older than the most ancient of their predecessors in the vales of Piedmont. So, too, may we say of the Lollards, Henricians, Paterines, Paulicians, Donatists, and other ancient Baptists, that they claim an origin more ancient than that of the men or the circumstances from which they derived their peculiar appellations. If in any instance the stream of descent is lost to human eye, in "the remote depths of antiquity," they maintain that it ultimately reappears, and reveals its source in Christ and his apostles.

Now we think that this singular unanimity of opinion among the Baptists of all countries and of all ages, respecting their common origin in apostolic and primitive times — a unanimity the existence of which might easily be established by numerous quotations from historians and other writers among them, is of itself a fact of no little value, as furnishing a presumptive argument of much force in support of the Baptist claim. In England and in the United States especially, the Baptists are now numerous, intelligent, and in every way as respectable as any denomination of Christian people. Among them are men, not only of unimpeachable moral and Christian character, but of profound learning and extensive historical research. And all these, as well as the humblest and most unlearned among them, believe that Baptists, (whether with or without the name, is a matter of indifference,) have existed "from the days of John the Baptist until now."

We readily concede that this mere opinion cannot of itself establish their claim to an apostolic origin. But, to all unprejudiced minds, it furnishes presumptive proof in favor of that claim. If on the part of any numerous and widely scattered race of men, there now existed, and for ages had existed, a tradition of a common origin, in some distant land, at a period remote, but fixed—a tradition, which all held, the philosophic historian would certainly not feel himself at liberty to disregard it. On the contrary, such tradition would receive his profoundest respect, and engage his most serious investigations. And if, with the tradition were found numerous traces of similarity of language, manners and customs, complexion, and general physiological character, between those holding it, and those from whom they professed to have sprung, still stronger would be the presumption in favor of its truth.

And why should not a similar tradition, similarly held, by numerous widely-scattered, intelligent Christian communities of the same spiritual race—communities not at all given to boasting of men, or of any outward circumstances whatever—accompanied too by the clearest and strongest evidences of similarity, not to say identity, in all essential characteristics, between themselves and those from whom they profess to have derived their origin, receive equal respect and consideration?

But the Apostolic origin of the Baptists is not a matter of tradition or of opinion, however universal and however strong. It is a matter of history — the highest history — history written by the hand of man, yet guided and inspired by God. Passing over the traditions and opinions of men, whether themselves or others,—passing over all mere human history, they go, for the proof of their apostolic origin, at once to the only infallible source of evidence upon the subject. They appeal to the divine record itself; and in that they find the fullest and most satisfactory vindication of their claims.

Just before his ascension, Jesus said to his apostles, "All power is given unto me in heaven and in earth. Go ye, therefore, and teach all nations, baptizing them in the name of the Father, and of the Son, and of the Holy Ghost: teaching them to observe all things whatsoever I have commanded you: and lo, I am with you alway, even unto the end of the world. Amen."—Matt. xxxviii. 18, 19, 20. Or, as Mark renders his words, "Go ye into all the world and preach the Gospel to every creature. He that believeth and is baptized, shall be saved; but he that believeth not shall be damned."—Mark xvi. 15, 16. Here is furnished the authority under which the Apostles acted in proclaiming and establishing the kingdom of Christ among the nations. Nothing is easier than to show that it called for the establishment of Baptist churches, and that the apostles and evangelists, faithfully fulfilling its provisions, actually established such churches. Under the requirements of the divine charter which guided and governed their procedure, they were, 1. To preach the gospel to every creature—to every creature capable of understanding and receiving the glad tidings which they proclaimed. Thus preaching, they were, 2. To make disciples of their hearers—to secure their assent to, and acceptance of, the glad tidings which they proclaimed. 3. They were to baptize those thus believing and accepting the gospel. 4. They were to go on teaching them to observe all things whatsoever Christ had commanded.

In this simple analysis of the commission is presented the very process by which Baptists are now made, constituted into churches, and governed. That it was the process by which the first preachers made converts, and constituted churches, is beyond question. The inspired historian tells us that while Peter preached on the day of Pentecost, his hearers "were pricked in their hearts, and said unto Peter and to the rest of the apostles, Men and brethren, what shall we do? Then Peter said unto them, Repent and be baptized, every one of you in the name of Jesus Christ. * * Then they that gladly received the word were baptized: and the same day there were added unto them about three thousand souls. And they continued steadfastly in the apostles' doctrine and fellowship, and in breaking of bread, and in prayers."—Acts ii. 37–42. He also tells us that "when Philip went down to the city of Samaria, and preached Christ to them, the people with one accord gave heed unto those things which Philip spake, hearing and seeing the miracles which he did." And "when they believed Philip preaching the things concerning the kingdom of God, and the name of Jesus Christ, they were baptized, both men and women."—Acts viii. 5–12.

Who does not see that these early converts, made by this divine process, whether called disciples, as at first, or Christians, as subsequently at Antioch, could have been nothing else than Baptists? For, consider 1. That they were *men and women*—that no infants are either directly named, or indirectly suggested even. 2. That they repented and believed *before* they were baptized. 3. That they were baptized before they "were added" to the company of the disciples—to the church. 4. That they were *added to the church* before they "broke bread," or partook of the Lord's Supper. If we have not here all the elements of a Baptist church, as constituted in the present day, then we think they are not to be found in such a church itself.

That the baptism which these early Christians received in declaration of their faith, was *immersion*, is evident from the following considerations:

1. The *meaning of the term defining the rite.*—The word always employed to denote the baptismal action, is Βαπτίζω, or some of its immediate inflections. And it uniformly and essentially involves, *both in classic and in Hellenistic usage*, the idea of an immersion. This, whatever sciolists and partisans may say, the scholarship of the world, Pedobaptist as well as Baptist, has put beyond all question. The most distinguished scholars of every age, and of all theological creeds, concede it. And, even if, in this brief essay, in which so many other topics are to be touched, we had the space, it were a work of supererogation to attempt a new and independent argument in proof of it.

2. The *symbolic import of the rite.*—In baptism is represented the plunging of the guilty and polluted soul into the fountain opened in the house of David for sin and for uncleanness, and the washing of regeneration through the power of the Holy Ghost. A complex symbol, in it is also represented the death, burial, and resurrection of Christ; the death and burial to sin of the believer,

his resurrection to newness of life, and his faith in the resurrection and future felicity of the bodies of all departed believers. And surely no act could be more significant of these things, than that of the immersion in water of the believer. None could be less so, than that of sprinkling or pouring water upon the unconscious, unbelieving, unconsenting babe.

3. The *scriptural representations*, in some instances remarkably circumstantial and minute, of *baptismal scenes.*—Matthew, speaking of the first baptism, says: "Then went out to him [John the Baptist] Jerusalem and all Judea, and all the region round about Jordan, and were baptized of him *in Jordan*, confessing their sins."—Matt. iii. 5, 6. Mark, speaking of the same baptismal scene, says: "John did baptize in the wilderness, and preach the baptism of repentance for the remission of sins. And then went out unto him all the land of Judea, and they of Jerusalem, and were all baptized of him *in the river of Jordan*, confessing their sins."—Mark i. 4, 5. Matthew, speaking of the baptism of Jesus, says: "Then cometh Jesus from Galilee to Jordan unto John, to be baptized of him. * * And Jesus, when he was baptized, went up straightway out of the water."—Matt. iii. 13–16. Mark, recording it, says: "And it came to pass in those days, that Jesus came from Nazareth of Galilee and was

baptized of John *in Jordan*. And straightway coming up out of the water, he saw the heavens opened," etc.—Mark i. 9, 10. John the Evangelist, after referring to Jesus and his disciples as baptizing in the land of Judea, says of John the Baptist, that he "also was baptizing in Enon, near to Salim, *because* there was *much water* there."—John iii. 2, 3. And Luke, in Acts, describing the baptism of the Ethiopian eunuch by Philip says: "As they went on their way, they *came unto a certain water:* and the eunuch said, See, here is water, what doth hinder me to be baptized? And Philip said, If thou believest with all thy heart thou mayest. And he answered and said, I believe that Jesus Christ is the Son of God. And he commanded the chariot to stand still: and *they went down both into the water*, both Philip and the eunuch, and he baptized him. And when *they were come up out of the water*, the Spirit of the Lord caught away Philip that the eunuch saw him no more; and he went on his way rejoicing."—Acts viii. 36–40.

4. The *terms in which, as a symbolic burial and resurrection, the rite is alluded to* by the inspired writers. "Know ye not," says Paul to the Romans, "that so many of us as were baptized into Jesus Christ were baptized into his death? Therefore *we are buried with him by baptism* into death, that like as Christ was raised up from the

dead, by the glory of the Father, even so we also should walk in newness of life. For if we have been planted together in the likeness of his death, we shall be also in the likeness of his resurrection."—Rom. vi. 3–6. The same figure of a *burial and resurrection in baptism* he also employs when addressing his Colossian brethren: "Buried with him in baptism," says he, "wherein also ye are risen with him through the faith of the operation of God who hath raised him from the dead."—Col. ii. 12. Urging upon them, too, the argument from consistency, he says: "If ye, then, be risen with Christ [as in your baptism ye symbolically declared,] seek those things," etc.—Col. iii. 1.

That the churches constituted by the Apostles were regarded as *essentially spiritual, and composed of converted or regenerate and believing persons only*, is evident from the manner in which they are addressed and referred to as "believers," "saints," "the quickened," "the faithful," "the redeemed," "the sanctified," "the saved," etc. And so evident is it, that whenever and wherever the great and destructive error of admitting infants and other unconverted persons into the church, has prevailed, there has always been the notion of a regeneration, as more or less closely connected with their baptism and initiation.

That, too, the apostolic churches gathered by the process, and composed of the elements which we have indicated, were *local bodies*, outwardly and formally *independent one of another*, *separate from the State*, endowed by Christ with all the powers, and *performing under him all the functions of sovereign, self-controlling bodies*, is evident from the way in which they are referred to throughout the New Testament. They are spoken of individually, as "the church at Jerusalem," the church at Antioch," "the church of the Ephesians," "the church in Smyrna," "the church which is in Nymphas' house," "every church." They are spoken of collectively, as "the churches," "the churches of Judea," "the churches of Galatia," "the churches of Macedonia," "the churches of Asia," "the churches of God," "the churches of Christ," "all the churches." They are represented as electing their own officers, admitting members to their fellowship and communion, expelling and restoring offenders, and, in a word, exercising all the powers lying legitimately within the province of distinct, self-governing, and independent Christian communities. That this was so, Mosheim, Gieseler, Neander, Schaff, and all the great ecclesiastical historians, distinctly show. An archbishop of the church of England thus strongly sets forth the fact: "It appears plainly from the sacred narrative, that though the many churches which the apostles founded were branches of one spiritual brotherhood, of which the Lord Jesus

Christ is the Heavenly Head—though there was "one Lord, one faith, one baptism," for all of them, yet they were each a distinct, independent community on earth, united by the common principles on which they were founded, and by their mutual agreement, affection, and respect, but not having any recognized head on earth, or acknowledging any sovereignty of one of these societies over others. And as for so-called general councils, we find not even any mention of them, or allusion to any such expedient. The pretended first council at Jerusalem does seem to me a most extraordinary chimera, without any warrant whatever from sacred history."[1]

That the churches thus independent of each other were independent of the State, is also clear. It is implied by Christ's declaration, "My kingdom is not of this world;" his injunction, "Render unto Cæsar the things that are Cæsar's, and to God the things that are God's;" the declaration of Peter and John to the Jewish rulers, when they commanded them not to speak at all, nor to teach in the name of Jesus, "Whether it be right in the sight of God to hearken unto you more than unto God, judge ye; for we cannot but speak the things which we have seen and heard;" and also

[1] Whately. Kingdom of Christ, p. 36. This testimony of Whately and others might be added to, were it necessary, almost *ad infinitum*.

from the uniform conduct of all the apostles and early Christians, who, while constantly rendering obedience to the civil government when acting within its legitimate sphere, as constantly resisted and defied its utmost power, when, presumptuously stepping outside of that sphere, it invaded the spiritual domain of Christ and his churches, and interfered with the rights and responsibilities of conscience.

That the first churches admitted to the Lord's table only such as had been, upon profession of faith, baptized into their fellowship, is also evident—so evident that no one of any Christian denomination questions it. Even Robert Hall, while strongly contending that there is no essential connection of baptism with the Lord's Supper, or any natural and necessary dependence of the latter upon the former, yet grants that "the apostles admitted none to the Lord's Supper, but such as were previously baptized,"[1] and concedes "the prior claim of baptism to the attention of such as are properly enlightened on the subject."[2]

In addition to the points of agreement—the evidences of identity, between the apostolic churches and the Baptist churches of the present day, to which we have directed attention, we may

[1] Hall's Works, vol. ii, pp. 213, 214.
[2] Ibid. vol. i. p. 310.

also name that of remarkable similarity in their *modes and forms of worship.* Like the present Baptists, and unlike many of those who so proudly vaunt that they are their only true descendants and successors, the apostolic churches were distinguished for the plainness and simplicity of their worship. They had no magnificent cathedrals, no gorgeously arrayed priesthood, no prescribed ritual, no splendid religious shows, no pomp of music, no parade of images and paintings—nothing to delight the mere imagination or the senses. Quietly and unostentatiously they met in some "upper room," or other humble sanctuary, to sing God's praise, supplicate his favor, read and expound his word, exhort one another, and, in all kindred ministries, to exercise and cultivate the spiritual gifts and graces which God had bestowed upon them.

To this model, the worship of the Baptists is conformed. Their ministers, though often learned and able, are for the most part plain and practical men, whose taste as well as sense of duty, prompts them to dispense the truth simple and unadorned, without the aid of the enticing words of man's wisdom, or other adventitious and carnal helps, which give to the public ministrations of so many others their chief attractions. There is nothing in the appendages and concomitants of any of their modes and forms of worship, more than in their general strain of preaching, to take captive the imaginative and the dreamy, the man of sentiment and the woman of fashion—nothing to attract the poetaster, the dilettante, and the trancendentalist —nothing to fascinate those to whom religion is but a fine art, or an assemblage of fine arts—whose devotion is but the glow of a poetic temperament, the expression of mere natural sentiment—homage to music, and architecture, and painting; a luxurious spiritualized indulgence of the imagination and the senses,—nothing to secure the homage of those devout worshipers of brick and mortar, and stucco and stone, and holy ground, who in some places have appropriated to themselves the high-sounding title of *Ecclesiologists.*

Here we have, as we think, a demonstration that the apostolic and primitive churches of Christ were in all essential respects identical with those of the modern Baptists. If there be any important difference between them, we are unable to perceive it. And we respectfully submit that in view of this identity, the latter have a right to claim that they are the true representatives and proper successors of the former, without being under any real necessity of tracing a chain of succession, and showing that no single link is wanting in that chain. Many a link in the deep darkness of the long and dreary past, amidst its revolutions and convulsions, may have been visible to the eye of God, nay, to the eyes of men then living, yet invisible to ours. For many centuries we have no connected and complete history of certain nations of marked peculiarities. Who doubts their continued existence throughout every hiatus in their history? For many ages there was no written history of the human race. Yet who doubts the existence of the race? It existed as really and certainly during all the unrecorded centuries, as during the historic ages. Its existence was in no manner dependent either upon the knowledge or the ignorance of men unborn. The first man, Adam, stood at one end of the line—another man, *just like him*, stood at the other. Is it difficult to believe, however wide and dark the interval which separated them, that the latter was the true and proper successor of the former? So the churches of the apostolic age stand at one end of the ecclesiastical line, the Baptists *just like them*, stand at the other. Why doubt that the line has been continuous,—though we may, in the darkness, or because of our own defective vision, be unable to see its whole extent,—and that those who stand at this end, are the true descendants and successors of those who stand at that?

In all consistency and candor, we think their Pedobaptist opponents, whatever others may think of it, should grant the validity and force of this reasoning in support of the Baptist position. They cannot at all trace the existence of infant baptism for a long period subsequent to the apostolic age. They contend, however, that having at the first existed, its continuance is to be presumed during all the long interval in which no trace of it is found. And if the existence of infant baptism *at the first*, were, as it is not, proved, we should unhesitatingly concede the strength of the presumption in its favor. The Baptists, as we have seen, *can* and *do prove* their existence in the apostolic age. If then, there were really a wide hiatus in their history, the just principle upon which (in a wrong application of it, however,) their Pedobaptist opponents proceed, would enable them at once to fill it.

Justly, as well as with great strength and felicity of expression, one of our brethren says, "Whatever is *found* in the New Testament is as worthy as if you traced it there. It is only a doubtful practice whose thread must be traced thus carefully through the labyrinth of history, with painful uncertainty lest you reach its end, while yet a century or two from Christ. If between us and the apostolic age there yawned a fathomless abyss, into whose silent darkness intervening history had fallen, with a Baptist church on this side, and a New Testament on the other, we should boldly bridge the gulf, and look for the record of our faith among the hills of Galilee."[1]

[1] Rev. J. Wheaton Smith.—Letter to Mr. Barnes.

III.

CONTINUITY OF THE BAPTISTS.

Inability to trace Historic Connection with Primitive Churches charged against the Baptists False theory of Succession—True Succession and Continuity claimed by the Baptists—Disadvantages under which they labor in Tracing their History—The Difficulties not Insuperable—Faithful Witnesses for God in all Ages—Statement of President Edwards—Those to whom he refers for most part Baptists—Opinion of Sir Isaac Newton—First Churches Baptist—Gradual Corruption—Rise of Antichristian Hierarchy—Opposition to it—The Novatians—The Donatists—The Paulicians—The Paterines—The Waldenses—German and Dutch Baptists—English and American Baptists—Recapitulation—Munster—Roger Williams.

AS is intimated in the preceding section, it is charged against the Baptists that while they claim essential identity with the apostolic and primitive churches, and from that identity consider themselves their true representatives and successors, they are wholly unable to trace any actual historic connection with them; that even if it be conceded that their churches have a certain outward conformity to the apostolic model, still nothing is gained, inasmuch as that conformity, in so far as it exists, is only *incidental* and *accidental*—an *irregular conformity*-and that there is no way in which they can satisfactorily establish their claim to a true apostolicity, but by tracing an uninterrupted clerical and ecclesiastical succession from the apostles and primitive churches of Christ.

This objection involves *a theory of succession* which invests the administration of baptism and the imposition of hands, with a "mysterious virtue," supposed to pass in unobstructed flow, and in a particular channel, from the apostles to their successors in every age, to which the Baptists have never subscribed ; but which they have always regarded as unscriptural and absurd.

Long since should this theory of the *jus divinum* of priests, have perished with its kindred theory of the *jus divinum* of kings. Like that, in looking at the outward and the formal alone or mainly, it proves itself repugnant to the very genius and spirit of Christianity, as well as at variance with the common sense of men. It assumes that the Divine Ruler having once employed a certain class of agents to effect his purposes, must needs continue them, or formal and strictly lineal successors of them, forever, having no power to transfer honor and authority from them to others not of their lineage—an assumption accordant neither with the divine character, nor the modes of the divine procedure. For how often has God suddenly and violently cast down one, and set up another in his place! How often has he taken the power from one dynasty and given it to another! He rejected Saul and gave the kingdom to David. He rejected the Jews and gave the gospel to the Gentiles.

If this theory be just, it will apply to things natural as well as spiritual. Does it? Is genius a matter of uninterrupted succession? From whom did the tinker of Elstow and the ploughman of Ayrshire derive the gifts which have made their names forever illustrious? Is patriotism a matter of such succession? May not a man love his country unless he be in the line of unbroken descent from a Codrus or a Curtius, an Alfred or a Tell? May not an amiable and gentle Pocahontas be the daughter of a savage and blood-thirsty Powhatan? May not a man be a fool whose father was a philosopher? Nay, may not a man be a philosopher whose father was a fool? But if in things natural, there may be the perpetuation of principle and spirit, the essence, the heart, the life, without absolute outward regularity, why may there not be in things spiritual? Is not the God of the natural economy, the same with the God of the spiritual? And are not the essential principles of his government and procedure identical in all its departments, even in those apparently the most diverse?

Essentially materialistic, this theory of succession, when consistently carried out, applies to consecrated *places* as well as to consecrated *persons.* It requires tactual succession and perpetuity in the latter as well as in the former. But the God who was purely worshiped in the plain and unimposing old tabernacle, and who filled it with his glorious presence, was just as acceptably worshiped in the magnificent temple which Solomon reared, where burned the Shekinah, and where was enshrined the divine oracle. And he who so honored the first temple, yet more highly honored the second, by that brighter and more glorious Shekinah, the actual presence of him who was the brightness of the Father's glory and the express image of his Person, and by that fuller and clearer oracle, the mouth of him who spake as never man spake. Were then the foundations of the first temple laid with portions of the old tabernacle? Did the simplicity and comparative rudeness of the latter, furnish the complete model for the symmetry and beauty, the grandeur and magnificence of the former? In building the second temple was it imperatively required to have the identical site, to the square yard and the square inch of the first? Were its completed walls but the continuation of the old walls, portions of which still standing, had alike defied the ruthless hand of Nebuchadnezzar, and the ravages of the mightier destroyer, Time.

There is no evidence from the Holy Scriptures

of either the truth or the necessity of this doctrine of "uninterrupted succession." It surely is not furnished by Christ's declaration, in the commission, "Lo! I am with you alway, even unto the end of the world." That is only the assurance of his presence with the heralds of the gospel, wherever they might go, or whatever they might do, in accordance with his will. Nor is such evidence furnished by Christ's declaration to Peter, "On this rock I will build my church, and the gates of hell shall not prevail against it." The notion that it is, proceeds from that papal and unscriptural assumption in which is involved the double error of confounding the church universal and invisible, with the visible church, and of supposing it to be founded upon Peter, rather than upon that eternal and immutable truth in which the apostles, through Peter, their spokesman, professed their faith—upon the weakness and instability of man, rather than upon the strength and immutability of God. When Christ said he would build his church upon a rock, he spoke, of course, figuratively. It would be subversive of the true principles of language and of all just rules of interpretation, to suppose that by the words he employed he meant to convey the idea that he would build a literal structure. Such a supposition would involve an incongruous mixture of ideas and of figures—such as a physical superstructure upon a spiritual foundation. The church which Christ affirmed that he would build, upon the spiritual foundation to which he referred, was a spiritual house, built up of living stones. And when he declared that the gates of hell should not prevail against it, he simply affirmed that the gates of hell should never prevail against the *essential principles* and *spirit* of the gospel, which are the life, the soul, of the church. That the gates of hell should not prevail against his church as an immortal energy, a heavenly spirit, a divine institution in the world.

Christ did, indeed, establish an outward and visible church, or perhaps we should rather say that he *gave to his church visibility.* But surely he did not mean that the gates of hell should never prevail against that mere visibility. Visibility is but a *circumstance* of the church, regarded in the sense in which Christ spoke of it. It must have existence before it can appear. It may still exist while vailing itself and withdrawing from human view—as when represented by "the woman in the wilderness," it existed for ages in obscurity, an obscurity so deep as that its very existence was then by the great world unknown, and is now with difficulty traced. The church to which Christ referred, first became visible as an outward local organization at Jerusalem. Now, if we admit that when Christ affirmed that the gates of hell should not prevail against it, he meant its visibility, or the outward organization in which for the time it enshrined itself, and through which it first found external development, how shall we reconcile his declaration with well attested facts? What shall we say when that assembly is scattered by persecution, ceases to perform the functions of the church visible, and has no existence save in its "*membra disjecta*"? As a visible and local organization, where is the church first founded at Jerusalem? For long ages it has ceased to exist. But the church to which Christ referred in his declaration to Peter, still survives—defying now as ever the gates of hell. So with respect to ten thousand other outward forms in which the church universal, the true spiritual church of Christ, transmigrating, if we may be allowed so to speak, from age to age, and land to land, and thus developing a true and sublime metempsychosis, has enshrined itself, and through which it has been made visible. They, outward, physical, earthly, have passed away. That, immortal and divine, lives on with never-fading beauty, and undecaying strength.

If one point to the church of Rome, and say, there is *the church* to which, in his declaration to Peter, Christ referred, and against which, as an outward and visible organization, the gates of hell have never prevailed, we ask what right has that, more than any one of ten thousand other local ecclesiastical organizations, to claim to be the church of

Christ? If any one, more than another, of the visible churches which have existed, could claim to be, *par excellence*, THE CHURCH of Christ, the church referred to in the declaration to Peter, one would think it should be that *first established*, and of which Peter was one of the original and chief constituents. We grant that the church of Rome was once one of the many outward organizations through which the church universal, at different times and in different places, has been made visible—yet it was not the first. And it has long ceased to be such an organization at all. The gates of hell have prevailed against it—prevailed against it in the destruction of its original and essential character—the dissolution of its original and essential elements—the complete and absolute alteration of its relations to Christ—the reversal of its whole posture and aspect towards him. Nothing were easier than to show, by subjecting that body, in its present character and past history, to the infallible tests of the truth of God, that, whatever it may once have been, it is now no church of Christ at all. His truth has fled from it. His Spirit has forsaken it. It is the synagogue of Satan. It is the home and the seat of Antichrist. It is the habitation of dragons, a nest of every unclean bird. Its life is gone. It is but a huge and hideous corpse.

So far from the Scriptures sustaining this theory

of "uninterrupted succession," they show its utter futility. "Think not to say within yourselves," said John the Baptist to the ancient advocates of this theory, "we have Abraham to our father: for I say unto you that God is able of these stones to raise up children unto Abraham. And now also the axe is laid unto the root of the tree: therefore every tree which bringeth not forth good fruit is hewn down and cast into the fire." To the same class of persons Paul said, "He is not a Jew which is one outwardly; neither is that circumcision which is outward in the flesh: but he is a Jew which is one inwardly; and circumcision is that of the heart, in the spirit and not in the letter; whose praise is not of men, but of God."—Rom. ii. 17, 29. To those who said, "We be Abraham's seed," and, in virtue of their outward connection with the patriarch, claimed honors to which they were not entitled, Christ, pouring contempt upon this theory of succession, said, "If ye were Abraham's children ye would do the works of Abraham. * * Ye are of your father the devil, and the lusts of your father ye will do."—John viii. 39–44. To the woman of Samaria, saying to him, "Our fathers worshiped in this mountain, and ye say that in Jerusalem is the place where men ought to worship," he taught that it was not absolutely necessary to have connection with the outward and the formal in order to be recognized by God—not necessary to the acceptability of worship that it be offered either upon Mount Gerizim or Mount Zion, according to this or that prescribed form. "Woman," said he, "the hour cometh when ye shall neither in this mountain nor yet at Jerusalem, worship the Father. * * The hour cometh and now is when the true worshipers shall worship the Father in spirit and in truth, for the Father seeketh such to worship him. God is a Spirit, and they that worship him must worship him in spirit and in truth." To those who inquired of him "when the kingdom of God should come," he said, "The kingdom of God cometh not with observation. Neither shall they say, Lo, here! or Lo, there! for behold, the kingdom of God is within you." All unobserved, it was even then in their very midst. And very graciously, on one occasion, he said to his disciples, "Where two or three are gathered together in my name, there am I in the midst of them."

Far be it from us to disparage any, even the least, of the outward ordinances of God. We honor them and keep them. But outward ordinances are only important as they are the vehicles of something infinitely higher and better. This, indeed, God demonstrated, even under the first dispensation, intensely formal and ceremonial though it was. The new moons, and solemn feasts, and costly sacrifices, of those who had no

5

heart in his service, and who subordinated the spirit to the form, so far from being pleasing to God, were an abomination to him. He would have mercy and not sacrifice, justice and judgment rather than the fat of rams. One who had been reared under that dispensation, and who had been deeply imbued with its spirit, confessed to Christ (and was commended for it by him), that to love God "with all the heart, and with all the understanding, and with all the soul, and with all the strength, and to love his neighbor as himself, is more than all whole burnt-offerings and sacrifices." And to him who, under the old dispensation, inquired, "Wherewithal shall I come before the Lord, and bow myself before the high God? Shall I come before him with burnt-offerings, with calves of a year old? Will the Lord be pleased with thousands of rams, or with ten thousands of rivers of oil? Shall I give my first-born for my transgression—the fruit of my body for the sin of my soul?" comes the emphatic and significant response, "He hath showed thee, O man, what is good, and what doth the Lord require of thee but to do justly, to love mercy, and to walk humbly with thy God."

We wonder not, then, that this theory of "uninterrupted succession" finds no real support in the writings of the ablest and best of the Christian Fathers. That, though often quoted in support of it, many of them, Tertullian, Jerome, Ambrose, Gregory Nazianzen, Augustine, and others, repudiate it—all contending that succession of doctrine and of faith, of principle and spirit, is the only true succession, and that without it, however important outward and formal succession may be, when viewed in certain aspects, it is of no avail, and not worthy of regard—being often claimed by heretical teachers and apostate churches.[1] Nor do we wonder that Luther, Melancthon, Calvin, and all the leading Reformers should contemn it; that tho Presbyterian Turrettine, the Episcopalian Stillingfleet, and the great founder of Methodism, Wesley, as well as the Baptist Robinson, should ridicule it; that Archbishop Whately should ridicule it, too, pronounce it "absurd," and, in some of the conclusions to which it leads, even "impious;" that even Romish writers, while formally maintaining it, should, by its repugnance both to reason and to scripture, sometimes be constrained (as Turrettine shows, in a quotation from Bellarmine,) virtually to yield it. We only wonder that any, especially in these times, and in this country, and among professed Protestants, should be found to defend it.

The Baptists holding, then, in accordance with

[1] Vide Turrettini Opera, tom. iii., De Ecclesia : Quæst. i. et Quæst. xiii.

the common sense of men, in accordance with the teachings of the most illustrious of the early Fathers, the Reformers, and other eminent servants of God; above all, in accordance with the teachings of inspired men and of Christ himself, that the true succession is succession of principle, of spirit, of faith, and of works, maintain that the genuine representatives of the primitive Christians, the true successors of the apostles, are those who hold their doctrines, follow their example, tread in their footsteps; that it does not matter that there was once a time when one was not in the apostolic path, nor *when* nor *how* he got into it. If he be only in it now, that is enough—he is their successor. That, on the other hand, it does not matter that one was once in that path, nor when nor how he got out of it. If he be *not in it now*, he is not their successor. As many a one has begun right and ended wrong, so many a one has commenced wrong and ended right. To the proposition of his Romish opponent, that "want of succession of bishops and pastors holding always the same doctrine, and of the forms of ordaining bishops and priests which are in use in the Roman church, is a certain mark of heresy," admirable is the reply of the great Chillingworth, himself an Episcopalian, and at one time a Papist: "Nothing but want of truth, and holding error, can make or prove any man or church heretical.

For if he be a true Aristotelian, or Platonist, or Pyrrhonian, or Epicurean, who holds the doctrine of Aristotle, or Plato, or Pyrrho, or Epicurus, although he cannot assign any that held it before him for many ages together; why should I not be made a true and orthodox Christian, by believing all the doctrine of Christ, though I cannot derive my descent from a perpetual succession that believed it before me. * * What is more certain, than that he may make a straight line, who hath a rule to make it by, though never man in the world had made any before? And why, then, may not he that believes the Scripture to be the word of God, and the rule of faith, regulate his faith by it, and consequently believe aright, without much regarding what other men either will do or have done?"[1]

In the same spirit Dr. Ripley says: "A church that came into existence yesterday, in strict conformity to the New Testament principles of membership, far away from any long-existing church or company of churches, and therefore unable to trace an outward lineal descent, is a true church of Christ—for Christianity is not a religion of circumstances, but of principles—while a church so-called, not standing on the apostolic principles of

[1] Works.—Charity Maintained by Catholics, vol. ii. pp. 375, 376, 377.

faith and practice, and yet able to look back through a long line up to time immemorial, may have never belonged to that body of which Christ is the Head."[1] Yet more fully and with rare elegance and ability are the views of the Baptists, upon this subject of succession, expressed by another distinguished Baptist. Referring to their churches, he says: "Amongst their sister churches they are related by sympathies and kind offices, but they own no subjection, and acknowledge no dependence either on cotemporary churches of their own country, or upon the churches of other lands or other times, except as those churches have held the same truth, clung to the same Head, and have exhibited the same spirit. * * They claim to hold directly of the ever-living, almighty, and omnipotent Spirit, and to lean, without the interposition of chains of succession and lines of spiritual descent, immediately and for themselves on the bosom and the heart of the Saviour, who pledged his presence to the end of the world, where two or three are gathered together in his name. To all pedigrees of a spiritual and priestly class, claimed by some Christians, we oppose the permanent presence and indefeasible priesthood of the great Melchisedec of our profession, without beginning of days or end of years; and we claim to come up

[1] Introduction to Crowell's Church Manual, p. 4.

out of the wilderness, stayed directly on Christ and leaning on our beloved. We touch, so to speak, his bare arm as our stay, without the intervention of the envelopes of any favored order or virtue running through a chain of spiritual conductors. Our graces are not transmitted, but taken direct from the Redeemer's own hand. Nothing short of a personal application to Christ, we suppose, will avail us in conversion; and nothing short of the personal presence of Christ will sustain us in the dying hour; and, as churches, we judge nothing short of the personal presence of the Lord can give energy to our preaching, validity to our ordinances, or life to our worship. If we have this, let others find, if they can, something better, holier, older, newer, and vaster. We know it not and seek it not."[1]

We have said thus much upon a topic which in itself does not deserve the consideration we have given it, to show the utter unreasonableness and injustice of the objection to the Baptists, based upon an alleged inability on their part to trace an uninterrupted clerical and ecclesiastical succession, as well as to rebuke an assumption based upon a mere figment, and altogether absurd and preposterous.

From all that we have said, however, it must

[1] Williams' Miscellanies, pp. 140, 141.

not be inferred that the Baptists do not claim any sort of succession or continuity from the Apostles. They do claim a real succession and continuity. But, as we have all along intimated, they do it not as at all necessary to the establishment of their character and standing as true and apostolic churches of Christ. They do it in reply to the taunting and contemptuous charge of recency of origin, so often brought against them by their opponents. They do it "on the ground of truth and historic fact." They do it in vindication of their noble ancestry, "that the stigma of ingratitude may not attach to themselves, nor those worthy ones be deprived of their honorable and blood-bought renown." For a far higher reason, they do it in humble and heartfelt acknowledgment of the love and power of Him who, in all ages, amid all the vicissitudes and perils of their trying fortunes, has so wonderfully and graciously watched over and preserved them and their principles.

The sum and substance of the Baptist claim to continuity from primitive times until the present, is simply this—that in all the intervening ages there have been persons, more or less numerous or conspicuous, existing as formally organized churches, or as scattered individuals, assembling from time to time, as their enemies allowed them opportunity, for the worship of God and for mutual edification—persons who, if now living, would be universally recognized as Baptists. If the existence, in all ages, of such persons, can be proved, all for which the Baptists contend will be proved. And that it can be, they at least have no doubt.

In tracing their continuity, the Baptists frankly confess that they encounter not a few difficulties. They labor under disadvantages which they think should not, in common fairness, be overlooked by their opponents. It might be expected that much labor would be necessary in collecting and bringing to bear upon the question, all the evidence which really exists. Much too, which it may reasonably be inferred once existed has been lost, and cannot now by any degree of labor and research be adduced at all. Since the origin of the Baptists, long and eventful ages have elapsed. Some of them were ages of great ignorance and darkness, in which facilities for collecting, preserving, and handing down to other times such records as are now desirable, were extremely limited. The printing-press had not been invented. Few could read, and yet fewer write. Not one in many thousands could compose a page that would survive him. Many of those ages, too, were periods of commotion and convulsion, of perpetual strife and contention, warfare and bloodshed, tyranny and oppression. Men were afraid to speak or to write—almost to think! During the progress of those long ages, the Baptists passed through many and great vicissitudes. They were in the minority. Their enemies sat in the seats of power. The principles for which the world is at length beginning to honor them, were then fiercely denounced as heresy and treason. If they ventured to publish them, their voices were hushed in death, or stifled in prison. Every effort that earthly malice or hellish hate could devise for the extermination of their principles was made. And had they not been immortal, all vestige of them, save in the records of the courts and councils which condemned as felons those who held and taught them, they would certainly have faded forever from the earth. "The Baptists had to conceal themselves like the innocent dove in the clefts of rocks and hollow trees to be secure from the talons of the hawk." Thus fleeing from their foes and concealing themselves, they continued for centuries in the deepest obscurity. Hence they have been almost entirely overlooked by many who have written *the history of the great antichristian hierarchy*, and called it *the history of the church of Christ*. If the Baptists could have written so freely and fully as their opponents, and if their writings could have been preserved, the work of tracing their history and establishing their claim to continuity, would now be comparatively slight. As it is, this is to be done chiefly through the writings of those who viewed every thing good concerning them "through the refracting medium of bitter enmity." Their opponents and persecutors held the pen as well as the sword. And these it is that make history. We need not say how in the hands of those who wielded them, they did their work.

"The Baptists," says Halbertsma, "existed several centuries before the Reformation, but then a history of them was an impossibility. It was ever the main condition of their existence to keep out of sight. Excluded from all ecclesiastical and civil offices, they could never appear in any of the State documents. Repudiating all the doctrines and ceremonies of the Romish Church which Jesus had not commanded, by this disavowal, they caused to disappear, all those distinctions in doctrines which separated the other sects. Since the kingdom of God was shut up in their bosoms, and was made known by no outward actions whatever, they existed by hundreds of thousands, as if not in existence, and only were known of men through the persecutions and investigations made by the Inquisition. Hence it is absurd to demand a series of historical truths, by which the existence of the earliest Baptists of the Reformation, and that of their spiritual ancestors in the middle ages, may be firmly bound together."[1]

[1] The Baptists and their Origin; Deventer, 1843, p. 226. See translation from the Dutch of S. Blaupot Ten Cate's Hist.

Nor must the peculiarity of their views of the nature and constitution of the church be overlooked in considering the question of the continuity of the Baptists. They have never acknowledged any visible and organized church universal. They have always contended that the people of God while, indeed, holding in common the great leading and essential principles of the Gospel, and being one in spirit, are, in so far as they sustain outward church relations, comprised in *churches*, rather than in *a church*. "It is not a *confederation* of Baptist churches," says a recent writer, "nor a continued *succession* of Baptist churches, that is the Baptist church; but every local independent body of baptized believers, holding the doctrines of the Gospel, and having the ordinances of the gospel, that now exists, or has at any time or in any place existed, is and was *the Baptist church* in the only sense in which there can be any such thing as the Baptist church." Their various communities, therefore, having always been separate and distinct bodies not formally united in one great ecclesiastical organization, were little likely, especially in such times as those to which we have referred, even when each one in its true sphere nobly fulfilled the purpose of God, to make themselves very conspicu-

Inq. into Waldensian Origin of Dutch Baptists. So. Bap. Rev. July, 1857.

ous or powerful in a worldly or historic point of view. It often, indeed, happened that those communities, from personal, local, and other incidental causes, bearing different appellations, though not different in faith, were regarded by the world and the established hierarchy, as well as by many learned historians, as *different sects,* when they were as properly but one people, as the different and widely-scattered churches of the apostolic age, or the different Baptist churches of this country now are. The proof is decided, that while the Baptists have been known by the many names of Baptists, Anabaptists, Waldenses, Albigenses, Petrobrussians, Henricians, Paulicians, Paterines, Donatists, Novatians, and Christians, they have ever been in principle and spirit really the same people.

Notwithstanding the disadvantages which exist, however, the tracing of the continued existence of the Baptists, is not so difficult as might at first view be expected. God, whose prerogative it is to bring good out of evil, and to make the wrath of man praise him, has caused the very enemies of his afflicted people, even in the act of striving to destroy them and blot out their name, bear unwilling and unwitting testimony to them. From those who spoke and wrote against them, from the tribunals which condemned them, from their judges and executioners, come both the history and the

6

eulogy of the Baptists. The courts which arraigned and tried them upon charges of heresy and treason, in some instances preserved records which reveal the fact that the faith of the heretic was the faith of the gospel,—his heresy, the truth as it is in Jesus.

Thus can the existence and continuity of the Baptists be traced. Traced by their sufferings for the truth—"by the stains of their martyrs' blood—by the light of their martyrs' fires"—by the broad wake of glory which followed them, as they moved on, in the darkness, through the deep waters of tribulation.

That there have been in all ages since the Apostles, persons who, when tried by the strictest scriptural tests, approve themselves as the *proper representatives and successors of the first followers of Christ*, is acknowledged by all. President Edwards speaking of the long and dreary interval between the rise of Antichrist and the Reformation, with his usual power of condensation and force of statement, says, "In every age of this dark time, there appeared particular persons in all parts of Christendom, who bore a testimony against the corruptions and tyranny of the Church of Rome. There is no one age of Antichrist, even in the darkest times of all, but ecclesiastical historians mention a great many by name who manifested an abhorrence of the Pope, and his idolatrous worship, and pleaded for the ancient purity of doctrine and worship. God was pleased to maintain an uninterrupted succession of witnesses through the whole time, in Germany, France, Britain, and other countries,—as historians demonstrate, and mention them by name, and give an account of the testimony which they held. Many of them were private persons, and many of them ministers, and some magistrates, and persons of great distinction. And there were numbers in every age, who were persecuted and put to death for this testimony."[1]

The Baptists claim, whether President Edwards would have conceded it or not, that the persons to whom he refers, were, for the most part, substantially Baptists. And this claim we think they can and do establish, as we shall soon see. Not now to adduce the testimony of others, we will only say, in passing, that that illustrious Christian philosopher, Sir Isaac Newton, whose ecclesiastical investigations were only less extensive and profound than his philosophical, frequently expressed to Whiston, as the latter states in the memoirs of his own life, his conviction that "the Baptists were the only Christians who had never symbolized with the Church of Rome."[2]

We have seen that the first churches were Bap-

[1] Works, vol. i. p. 460.

[2] See Robert Hall's Works, vol. i. p. 358.

tist churches. Such they continued throughout the apostolic age, and indeed in all fundamental and essential respects, for a considerable period afterward, as we might easily show by an appeal to Mosheim, Neander, Bunsen, and other writers of the highest authority. Gradually, however, the purity of their doctrine was corrupted, and the strictness of their discipline relaxed, signs of which had already appeared, even in the age of the apostles themselves. Multitudes of errorists and pretended converts were admitted into the churches, until at length these outnumbered the true people of God, and obtained the control of affairs. This was especially the case in the time of Constantine, the Emperor, and Sylvester, the Bishop of Rome, under whom, in the early part of the fourth century, the church and the state were united. From this time, the general declension and defection were very deep and rapid. The churches became more and more superstitious in their worship, and introduced many unscriptural and heathenish ceremonies into the service of God's house. They "brought in the worship of saints, and set up images in their places of worship, and the clergy in general, and especially the Bishop of Rome, assumed more and more authority to himself. In the primitive times he was only a minister of a congregation ; then a standing moderator of a presbytery ; then a diocesan bishop; then a metropolitan, which is equivalent to an archbishop; then he was a patriarch; then afterward he claimed the power of universal bishop over the whole Christian church through the world, wherein he was opposed for a while, but afterward confirmed in it by the civil power of the Emperor in the year 606. After that he claimed the power of a temporal prince, and so was wont to carry two swords, to signify that both the temporal and spiritual sword was his, and claimed more and more authority till at length he, as Christ's vicegerent on earth, claimed the very same power that Christ would have if he was present on earth, and reigned on his throne; or the same power that belongs to God, and used to be called *God on earth*."[1]

In the early part of this period, even at Rome itself, as well as in other portions of the empire, when the constantly-encroaching irregularities and ever-increasing corruptions threatened utterly to destroy the simplicity that is in Christ, and to subvert the essential principles of the gospel, those who remained steadfast in the true doctrine, and pure in life, and who from the first had resisted these irregularities and corruptions, and patiently borne with the abuses which they deplored, but had no power to correct, hopeless of reform, after many a struggle, at length overcoming their aversion to

[1] See Edward's Works, Hist. Red., vol. i. 457, 458.

separation, withdrew and established themselves in distinct and independent communities, in which, earnestly contending for the faith once delivered to the saints, they stemmed the swelling tides of error. These communities in different places, and under different appellations, continued to exist throughout all the dark and dreadful days of persecution which followed, until the Reformation, when, in their descendants and successors, they rose up simultaneously in great numbers, and asserted themselves in almost all parts of Europe. Since then, passing through great and trying vicissitudes, they have still held on their way, until increased in numbers, and otherwise greatly strengthened, they are now, *as Baptists,* known and acknowledged throughout the world.

The first important class, passing by the Montanists, with whom Tertullian identified himself, which openly resisted and organized themselves against the corruptions of the dominant party, were the Novatians. They received this name about the middle of the third century, and flourished until about the middle of the fifth. "Afterward," says Robinson, "when penal laws obliged them to lurk in corners and worship God in private, they were distinguished by a variety of names, and a succession of them continued until the Reformation." The same author styles them "Trinitarian Baptists."

The enemies of the Novatians have given them a very bad name. But to the loftiness of their principles, the strictness of their discipline, and the purity of their lives, Mosheim, Dupin, Adam Clark, Lardner, and others bear ample testimony.

"The rise of these puritans at so critical a period," says the historian Orchard, "their soundness in the faith, their regard to character and purity of communion, their vast extent and long success, must have had a powerful influence in all the vicinity of their churches in checking the ambition and secularity of the established clergy, and in shedding a moral auspice on benighted provinces. These sealed witnesses, (Rev. iii. 3,) were the first protestant dissenters from assuming hierarchies; and it is most gratifying to be able to *prove ourselves* the successors of a class of men who first set the example of contending for the purity and simplicity of Christian worship and a firm adherence to the laws of the King of Zion."[1]

After the Novatians, followed the Donatists. They arose early in the fourth century, in Africa, were very numerous and powerful, and flourished for several centuries, when, like the Novatians, they were outwardly suppressed by their enemies, and forced into exile and obscurity. But they still continued to exist. "For a thousand years

[1] History of Foreign Baptists, p. 63.

after the rise of the Donatists," says Benedict, "we find them spread along in all parts of Europe, under different names, but recognized by friends and foes as substantially the same people."[1]

The Donatists, like the Novatians, have been painted by their enemies in the most repulsive colors. But they were almost infinitely superior to those by whom they have been disparaged. And while we may regret any imperfections attaching to their character and conduct, we are not ashamed to recognize them as brethren, and to claim them, for the most part, as essentially Baptists. That they were such is evident. They immersed their converts, refused to baptize infants, opposed the union of church and state, preserved purity of discipline, simplicity of worship, and earnestly insisted upon holiness of life. Of the correctness of these statements, Robinson, Jones, Orchard, Benedict, Curtis, and others, furnish evidence. Neander shows that they strenuously insisted upon the principle that the church could rightly consist only of the pure, and that all others should be separated from it. A principle which, as they developed and applied it, could not fail to conflict with infant baptism whenever and wherever practiced, and to exclude it. The same great historian also shows that the Donatists held other principles,

[1] Hist. of the Baptists, p. 11.

which are incompatible with infant baptism and its unfailing adjuncts and concomitants. They bore their testimony with emphasis against the employment of force in matters of religion, and "manfully asserted" the great doctrine of the individuality and freedom of the human soul. "Did the Apostles ever persecute any one, or did Christ ever deliver any one over to the secular power?" significantly asks the Donatist Petilian. "God created man free, after his own image. How am I to be deprived of that by human lordship which God has bestowed on me?" with equal significance inquires the Donatist Gaudentius.[1] Surely infant baptism, forestalling the individual judgment and the individual conscience, anticipating and violating the right of personal choice, and *making Christians* those who have never yielded their consent, could no more exist among these ancient Baptists than among their modern descendants and successors.

The learned Dr. Thomas Fuller, the author of a church history of Great Britain, which has been for nearly two hundred years in high estimation among English Episcopalians, speaking of certain Baptists, some of whom suffered martyrdom for their faith in the time of Henry VIII., says: "These Anabaptists, for the main, are but the

[1] See Neander's Hist. Ch. Rel. and Ch. vol. ii. pp. 203–217.

Donatists new-dipped."[1] Long, Prebendary of St. Peter's, says of the Donatists, that "they did not only re-baptize the adults that came over to them, but refused to baptize children, contrary to the practice of the church, as appears by several discourses of St. Augustine."[2] Twisck, Chron. bk. vi. p. 201, says, "The followers of Donatus were all one with the Anabaptists, denying baptism to children, admitting believers only thereto who desired the same, and maintaining that none ought to be forced to any belief." D'Anvers, in his Treatise on Baptism, says: "Austin's third and fourth books against the Donatists demonstrate that they denied infant baptism, wherein he managed the argument of infant baptism against them with great zeal, enforcing it by several arguments, but especially from apostolical tradition, and cursing with great bitterness them that should not embrace it. And therefore Osiander, in his Epit. Cent. 16, p. 175, saith that our modern Anabaptists were the same with the Donatists of old." Benedict says that H. Bullinger invariably identifies the Donatists with the Anabaptists, or as he styles them, *Baptists*. "They are," says Bullinger,

[1] Ch. Hist. of Britain, vol. ii. p. 96, ed. 1837—as quoted in True Union, Sept. 8, 1859.

[2] Hist. of Donatists, by Thomas Long, B. D. etc., Preb. St. Peter's, Exon. London, Walter Kettilby, 1677—as quoted in True Union.

"similar in every particular to the old Baptists," the Donatists.[1]

About the middle of the seventh century, the Paulicians, another party of Baptists, came into notice in the east, where, as in the west, the greatest errors and corruptions prevailed. Orchard calls them the "restorers of the New Testament order of things."

However defective the views and practices in some respects of many of them, through certain Gnostic and Mystic influences to which their peculiar circumstances exposed them, it is clear that they regarded the ordinances of baptism and the Lord's Supper as pertaining only to *believers*. "In the practice, or at least in the theory of the sacraments," says Gibbon, "the Paulicians were inclined to abolish all visible objects of worship; and the words of the gospel were, in their judgment, the baptism and communion of *the faithful*."[2] Mosheim, speaking of a certain class of these people, says that "they supposed all religion to consist in pious exercises, and in actions conformed to the law of God, while they despised all external worship." And he adds, "They rejected baptism as a rite of no use as regards salvation, and especi-

[1] See various authorities referred to by Benedict, pp. 64, 65, Hist. Baptists.

[2] Milman's Gibbon, vol. v. p. 388.

ally the baptism of infants."[1] Dr. Milner says that "they were simply scriptural in the use of the sacraments; they were orthodox in the doctrine of the Trinity; they knew of no other mediator than the Lord Jesus Christ."[2]

Dr. Allix, in his Remarks upon the Churches of Piedmont, says that "they were Anabaptists, or rejecters of infant baptism, and were consequently often reproached with that term." Robinson also gives the same account of them.

Like that of the churches of Greece, and, indeed, of all others of that time and for several centuries later, their baptism was immersion. After continuing until the eleventh century as distinct and independent communities, they were blended with the Waldenses and other kindred people.

Like the Paulicians, contemporary with them, and, as some suppose, deriving their origin from them, were the Paterines of Italy, though Robinson and Jones believe that they had always existed in that country. The former, upon the testimony of eminent Romish writers, to whose works he refers, says that they maintained that a Christian church ought to consist of only good people; that it had no right to frame any constitution, *i. e.* apart from the Scriptures; that a man ought not

[1] Murdock's Mosheim, vol. ii. p. 204.

[2] Ch. Hist. Cent. 9, ch. ii., as quoted in Orchard's For. Bap.

to be delivered up to officers of justice to be converted; that the benefits of society belong alike to all its members; that faith without works could not save a man; that the church ought not to persecute any, even the wicked. Their "public religion" consisted of nothing but social prayer, reading and expounding the gospel, baptism once, and the Lord's supper as often as convenient. Robinson still further says of them: "As the Catholics of those times baptized by immersion, the Paterines, by what name soever they were called, as Manicheans, Gazari, Josephites, Passagines, etc., made no complaint of the mode of baptizing, but when they were examined, they objected vehemently against the baptism of infants, and condemned it as an error: among other things, they said that a child knew nothing of the matter, that he had no desire to be baptized, and was incapable of making any profession of faith, and that the willingness of and professing of another could be of no service to him." Benedict says of the Paterines, that "besides their opposition to infant baptism, we see in their arrangement of associations a very distinct trait of their Baptist character."

The Paterines were of irreproachable life. And at one time they were so numerous as to be very formidable to their opponents. At length, however, they "were dispersed abroad into other provinces, or else they retired into obscurity, from either of which circumstances their local names would become extinct. The terror of the inquisitors awed the Italians into silence; but it is highly credible, indeed there are some reasons to believe, the Paterines did continue dispersed in Italy until the Reformation in Germany. It is very probable that many of these people became incorporated with the Waldensian churches in the valleys of Piedmont, which at this period enjoyed, under the Duke of Savoy, the sweets of religious liberty. This incorporation could be easily effected, since it is proved by Allix and others, that the most part of the Paterines held the same opinion as the churches in the valleys, and therefore were taken for one and the same people."[1]

The most important party, in some respects, which, during the dark ages, resisted the authority of Rome, were the Waldenses, who became more publicly and generally known when Peter Waldo, an opulent merchant of the city of Lyons, in France, connected himself with them and became their leader. "Many writers, both papal and Protestant, have most erroneously regarded him as the parent and founder of the proper Waldense. Mr. Robinson, however, has shown that this name has a much earlier origin, that it signifies "in-

[1] Foreign Baptists, p. 159.

habitants of the valleys,' and that it was applied to these persecuted people, simply for the reason that great multitudes of them made their residence in the valleys of the Alps and of the Pyrenees, where, age after age, they found an asylum from the tyranny of the church of Rome. This view of the matter, also, is supported by the testimony of their own historians, Pierre Gilles, Perrin, Leger, Sir Samuel Morland, and Dr. Allix. The names imposed upon them by their adversaries, they say, have been intended to vilify and ridicule them, or to represent them as new and different sects. Their enemies confirm their great antiquity. * * If we will believe the testimony of the suffering Waldenses themselves, their doctrine and discipline had been preserved, in all its purity and efficacy, from the days of the primitive martyrs, in Spain, France, Germany, Italy, and especially in the valleys of Piedmont."[1] President Edwards, after alluding to their obscure retreat, says: "It is supposed they first betook themselves to this desert secret place among the mountains, to hide themselves from the severity of the heathen persecutors which were before Constantine the Great. And there their posterity continued from age to age afterward. And being, as it were, by natural walls, as well as by God's grace, separated

[1] Encyc. Rel. Knowledge, Art. Waldenses.

from the rest of the world, never partook of the overflowing corruption."[1]

In his History of the Crusades against the Albigenses, M. Sismondi says: "Those very persons who punished the sectaries with frightful torments, have alone taken it upon themselves to make us acquainted with their opinions; allowing, at the same time, that they had been transmitted in Gaul from generation to generation, almost from the origin of Christianity. We cannot be astonished," he adds, "if they have represented them to us with all those characters which might render them the most monstrous, mingled with all the fables which would serve to irritate the minds of the people against those who professed them. Nevertheless, amidst many puerile and calumnious tales, it is still easy to recognize the principles of the Reformation of the sixteenth century among the heretics who are designated by the name of Vaudois, or Albigeois."

Reinerius, speaking of the Waldenses, or Poor Men of Lyons, uses the following remarkable language: "Of all the sects which have been or now exist, none is more injurious to the church [of Rome], for three reasons: 1. Because it is more ancient. Some aver their existence from Sylvester; others from the very times of the apostles.

[1] Edward's Works, vol. i., Hist. Red. p. 460.

2. Because it is so universal. There is scarcely any country into which this sect has not crept. And, 3. Because all other heretics excite horror by the greatness of their blasphemies against God; but these have a great appearance of piety, as they live justly before men, believe rightly all things concerning God, and confess all the articles which are contained in the creed; only they hate and revile the church of Rome, and their accusations are easily believed by the people."

"Here, then," in the language of the writer to whom we are indebted for several of the foregoing extracts, "is a succession of faithful men, whose apostolic origin, perpetuity, universal, though often hidden, diffusion, general orthodoxy, evangelical simplicity, and sanctity of character are admitted by the church of Rome herself; a succession of faithful men, organized into Christian churches, claiming to be the true successors of the apostles, protesting against all the corruptions of the patriarchate and the Papacy, and for this reason subject to continual persecution from both, through the hands of the secular powers to which they are allied; a church built not on St. Peter alone, but on the entire foundation of the apostles and prophets, Jesus Christ himself being the chief corner-stone, and against which the gates of hell have not been able to prevail."[1]

[1] Encyc. Rel. Knowl., Art. Waldenses.

And now the great question is,—Were these people Baptists? Several of the Protestant denominations seek their ancestry among them. We have no doubt that considerable diversity of faith and practice prevailed among the many communities who bore the name of Waldenses—an appellation which (like that of *Puritans*, in which both Baptists and Pedobaptists have often been included,) was employed with no little breadth and indefiniteness of signification. But that the old Waldenses proper, were, for the most part, essentially Baptists, seems to us so evident that we think, with Benedict, nothing but want of information, or partisan illiberality and unfairness, could ever have led to a denial of it. They held that the church of Christ is an assembly of godly persons; that its only rule of faith and practice is the word of God; that no one should be coerced in matters of conscience; that while the state is to be honored by "subjection, ready obedience, and the paying of tribute," it has no right to interfere with the internal administration of the church. They practiced immersion as baptism, and denied the rite to infants.

The evidence in support of this last statement has been sometimes questioned; but it is more than abundant. We are embarrassed, not by its deficiency, but by its excess. The Waldenses have always been charged with a denial of infant baptism. In the decrees of the Council of Toulouse, 1119, those of the second Lateran, 1139, and of the third Lateran, 1215, in the Decretals of Innocent III., and in numerous documents from the pens of others, they were charged with neglecting and opposing the baptism of infants. So far were they from denying it, that they put forth the strongest proofs of the justice of the charge. In the Treatise on Antichrist, Purgatory, Invocation of Saints, and the Sacraments, supposed to have been written by the celebrated Peter de Bruys, about the year 1120, in which are disclosed some of the more important views of the Waldenses, it is said of Antichrist, that "He teaches to baptize children into the faith, and attributes to this the work of regeneration; thus confounding the work of the Holy Spirit in regeneration with the external rite of baptism, and on this foundation bestows orders, and, indeed, grounds all his Christianity."[1]

In a full Confession of Faith, drawn up about the same time, they say, "We consider the sacraments as signs of holy things, or as the visible emblems of invisible blessings. We regard it as proper and even necessary that *believers* use these symbols, or visible forms, when it can be done. Notwithstanding, we maintain that believers may be saved without these signs, when they have

[1] Jones' Hist. Ch. Church, vol. ii. p. 51; N. Y. ed., 1824.

neither place nor opportunity of observing them."[1] In the "Noble Lesson," a work in verse, probably written about the year 1100, "they emphatically teach that the apostolic commission authorized the making and baptizing of 'disciples' only; that the apostles and primitive preachers baptized only believers; and that the first churches were composed of 'converts,' who 'trusted in Christ.'"[2] In addition to the Treatise on Antichrist, the Confession of Faith, and the Noble Lesson, the Waldenses put forth a catechism, a century or two later, in which "they strike at the very root of infant baptism, and assert the great principle of all Baptist peculiarity—*the church is a congregation of believers.*"[3] In "the public declaration of their faith to the French king, 1521," according to Montanus, the Waldenses "assert in the strongest terms the baptizing of believers, and deny that of infants."[4] So late as the year 1544, after some of their brethren, the ancestors of the present Waldenses, had been induced through the influence of the Reformers to compromise their ancient faith,[5]

[1] Jones' Hist. Ch. Ch., vol. ii. p. 43.

[2] Dr. Waller in Ch. Repos., Oct., 1858.

[3] Ib. ut sup.

[4] Twisck's Chron. p. 930. Merningus' Hist. Baptism, p. 739, as cited in Orchard's For. Bap., App. to Wald. Sect.

[5] "Following the teachings of the Scriptures, both Waldenses and Albigenses appear first universally to have rejected infant baptism and the use of oaths; but gradually, in the course of

they explicitly state in a Confession then drawn up and subscribed, "We believe that in the sacrament of Baptism the water is the visible and external sign which represents to us that which, by virtue of the invisible God so working, is within us; that is to say, the renovation of the Spirit and the mortification of our members in Jesus Christ; *by which also we are received into the holy congregation of God's people,* PROTESTING AND DECLARING BEFORE IT OUR FAITH AND CHANGE OF LIFE."[1] Jones

time, many of the Waldenses gave up these points. This occurred in a great degree at the time of the Reformation. They became acquainted with Zuingle, Œcolampadius and Bucerus, and the result was, a new Confession of Faith, which was made at Angrogne, in 1532. But they were not unanimous in the reception of this; and two of their teachers declared that it would be better to adhere to their former Confession, especially to that of the year 1100. But after that, there arose in the valleys a need of teachers; they turned to Geneva for aid, and reformed teachers taught in their midst, not using the language of the people, of which they were ignorant, but their native language, the French. As a matter of course, these preachers imparted their own peculiar views to the Waldenses. * * Since they do not reject infant baptism, and the use of oaths, as they formerly did, and since their young men who expect to enter the ministry, are instructed at the universities of Lausanne, Geneva, Montauban, Struatsburg, and Berlin, the peculiar opinions of the Baptists do not now prevail in their midst."—See Translation from S. Blaupot Ten Cate's Historical Inquiry: S. Bap. Rev., July, 1857.

[1] Hist. of Wald., Ed. by Dr. Baird, p 53, as quoted by Dr. Waller in Ch. Rep., Sep., 1858.

gives the latter part of this statement thus: "By this ordinance [baptism] we are received into the holy congregation of God's people *previously* professing and declaring our faith and change of life."[1]

Now, surely no better or fuller evidence than this could reasonably be required. For what can furnish more satisfactory information respecting the creed of a people than the creed itself? Other testimony in profusion is at hand. Our limits, however, allowing us to introduce only a very small portion of it, without any unnecessary minuteness of citation, we refer the reader who may wish to pursue the subject further, to the works of Robinson, Jones, Orchard, Benedict, and especially to a discussion of the Waldensian question by the late Dr. Waller, as published in Ch. Rep., Aug., Sept., Oct., Nov., Dec., 1858, in which the whole subject is treated with great ability, and the Baptist character of these ancient people of God, fully shown. We cite from these and other sources, only a few of the more modern authorities.

• Starck, Court preacher of Darmstadt, in his History of Baptism, says of the Waldenses, "If, instead of only looking at particular confessions, we follow out their general mode of thinking, we find that they not only rejected infant baptism, but

[1] Hist. Ch. Church, vol. ii. p. 47; N. Y. ed., 1824.

re-baptized those who passed from the Catholic church to them."[1]

M. de Potter, in a compendious account of the Waldenses, says, "They called the Pope Antichrist, opposed the payment of tithes, abolished the distinctions in the priesthood, denied the authority of councils, rejected all the ceremonies of baptism, except simple ablution; and laying stress on the truth that in infancy there can be no actual conversion to the Christian faith, they therefore baptized anew all those who left the Romish church, wishing to embrace their doctrine."[2]

One of the most celebrated barbs or pastors of the Waldenses, was Peter de Bruys. Mosheim says that he taught that persons "ought not to be baptized until they come to the use of reason."[3] Neander says "that he was an opponent of infant baptism, since *he regarded personal faith as a necessary condition for true baptism* and denied the benefit in the case of another's faith."[4]

Henry of Lausanne, the disciple of Peter, and like him a distinguished leader and teacher of the Waldenses, also rejected and opposed infant baptism. Neander says that "he attacked various customs which could not be directly proved from the Sacred Scriptures, as corruptions of primitive

[1] Hague's Hist. Disc., as quoted in Ch. Rep., Dec. 1858.

[2] Hague's Hist. Discourse.

[3] Murdock's Mosheim, vol. ii. p 267.

[4] Hist. Ch. Rel. and Church. vol. iv. p 595.

Christianity; such, for example, as the worship of saints, and infant baptism."[1] Mosheim says, "We only know that he too disapproved of infant baptism, inveighed severely against the corrupt morals of the clergy, despised the festal days and the religious ceremonies, and held clandestine assemblies."[2]

"It is certain," say Ypeij and Dermout, in their History of the Reformed Church of the Netherlands, "that the Netherlands' Waldenses always rejected infant baptism, and administered the ordinances only to adults. We may find this positively asserted respecting the Netherlands' Waldenses, by Hieronymus Verdussen, by the Abbot of Clugny, and other Romish writers. Hence it is that in this country they are better known by the name of Anabaptists, than by that of Waldenses."[3]

The author of the Historical Inquiry into the Waldensian origin of the Dutch Baptists says, "We are compelled to agree in opinion with Cornelius Van Huizen, who says that the Baptists in Switzerland and Alsatia had no other origin than the Waldenses." And he adds, "Vanizen considers

[1] Hist. Ch. Rel. and Church, vol. iv. p. 601.

[2] Murdock's Mosheim, vol. ii. p. 267.

[3] See Translation, So. Bap. Rev., April, 1859, of that portion of this History which refers to the Anabaptists and Baptists.

that many of the most distinguished Baptist families in Hamburg, Altona, and Embden, were of Waldensian origin." Again, says he, "Limborch who has accurately examined their opinions, in the Memorabilia of the Inquisition, at Toulouse, bears testimony respecting the Waldenses, that no Christians appear more closely to resemble them than those whom they call Mennonites,"—the Dutch Baptists.[1]

In the preface to the fifth edition, 1825, of his history of the Waldenses, Jones says, that "they brought up their children in the nurture and admonition of the Lord; but they neither sprinkled nor immersed them, under the notion of administering Christian baptism. They were, in a word, so many distinct churches of Anti-pedobaptists."

But why multiply proofs of what is so completely established? With the words of Robinson, the learned and able author of the History of Baptism, and of the Ecclesiastical Researches, we close what we now have to say upon this topic,—"Amidst all the productions of early writers, friends and foes,—confessors of the *whole* truth, and opposers of it, annalists, historians, recorders, inquisitors, and others, with the laboured researches of Usher, Newton, Allix, Collier, Wall, Perrin, Leger, Morland, Mosheim, Maclaine, Gilles, Sims, and others,

[1] See Translation from his work, in S. B. Rev., Oct. 1857.

all of the Pedobaptist persuasion, with every advantage of learning on their side, who collated councils, canons, synods, conferences, chronicles, decrees, bulls, sermons, homilies, confessions, creeds, liturgies, etc., from the private creed of Irenæus down to the rules of Augsburg,—who examined documents at home, and explored territories abroad,—their *united labors* could never produce a single dated document or testimony of Pedobaptism among the Vaudois, separate from the Romish community, from Novatian's rupture, to the death of the execrable monster, Alexander VI., 1503."

Other parties of Baptists, distinguished by different appellations, we have deemed it unnecessary particularly to mention. All held essentially the same principles, and were animated by the same spirit. "The different companies overlapped each other, and covered the whole ground; and notwithstanding all the persecutions, gibbets, and flames to which they were exposed, the interdicts, banishments, and exile, which were their never-ceasing portion, they continued in great numbers, down to the time of the Reformation."

To the great Waldensian faternity belonged the so-called German Anabaptists, and the Mennonites, or Dutch Baptists, to whose high antiquity and apostolic origin, testimony of the greatest weight by their opponents is borne. Cardinal Hosius, president of the Council of Trent, who as a Papist, certainly cannot be charged with being too favorable to them, affirmed that the Baptists, or Anabaptists as they were then called, had existed for twelve hundred years. Zuinglius, a little earlier, says, for *thirteen hundred years.* Twelve hundred years from the times of Zuinglius and Hosius, would carry the Baptists up to the fourth century—thirteen, up to the third—when immersion was universally practiced as baptism, save perhaps in a few cases of extreme illness; and when, although the Baptist principle of the independence of the churches was giving place to Episcopal pretensions and the establishment of a hierarchy, infant baptism, as Neander affirms, entered very rarely and with great difficulty, into the church life.[1]

The writer of the article on the Baptists, in the Edinburgh Encyclopædia, says—" It must have already occurred to our readers that the Baptists are the same sect of Christians which we formerly described under the appellation of Anabaptists. It is but justice to acknowledge that they reject the latter appellation with disdain, and maintain that as none of the forms adopted by other churches are consonant to Scripture, the baptism of those churches is in reality no baptism. Hence, in their opinion, they do not re-baptize. Indeed, *this seems*

Hist. Christ. Rel. and Ch., vol. ii. p. 319.

to have been their great leading principle, FROM THE TIME [A. D. 160–245] OF TERTULLIAN, [whom he elsewhere calls one of their 'earliest founders,'] to the present day."[1]

Mosheim, speaking of the Dutch Baptists, says, "The origin of the sect, who, from their repetition of the baptism received in other communities, are called Anabaptists, but who are also denominated Mennonites, from the celebrated man to whom they owe a large share of their present prosperity, is involved in much obscurity. For they suddenly started up, in various countries of Europe, under the influence of leaders of dissimilar characters and views; and at a time when the first contests with the Catholics so engrossed the attention of all, that they scarcely noticed any other passing occurrences." And he adds, that they "are not altogether in the wrong, when they boast of a descent from those Waldensians, Petrobrussians, and others, who are usually styled *the witnesses for the truth* before Luther. Prior to the age of Luther there lay concealed in almost every country of Europe, but especially in Bohemia, Moravia, Switzerland and Germany, very many persons, in whose minds was deeply rooted that principle which the Waldensians, the Wickliffites, and the Hussites maintained, some more covertly and others more openly;

[1] Ed. Encyc., Art. Baptists.

namely, that the kingdom which Christ set up on the earth, or the visible church, is an assembly of *holy* persons, and ought therefore to be entirely free not only from ungodly persons and sinners, but from all institutions of human device against ungodliness. This principle lay at the foundation, and was the source of all that was new and singular in the religion of the Mennonites [or Baptists]: and the greatest part of their singular opinions, as it is well attested, were approved some centuries before Luther's time, by those who had such views of the nature of the church of Christ."[1]

To the ancient and apostolic origin of the Baptists, the learned authors of the History of the Church of the Netherlands, a work prepared under royal patronage, in the early part of the present century, bear the most decided testimony. Stronger could not be desired. After having spoken at considerable length of the Baptists, they say,—"We have now seen that the Baptists who in former times were called Anabaptists, and at a later period, Mennonites, were originally Waldenses, who in the history of the church, even from the most ancient times, have received such a well deserved homage. On this account, the Baptists may be considered, as of old, the only religious community which has continued from the times of the Apostles—

[1] Eccles. Hist., Murdock's translation, vol. iii. pp. 198, 199, 200.

as a Christian society which has kept pure, through all ages, the evangelical doctrines of religion. The uncorrupted inward and outward condition of the Baptist community, affords proof of the truth, contested by the Romish Church, of the great necessity of a reformation of religion, such as that which took place in the sixteenth century, and also a refutation of the erroneous notion of the Roman Catholics, that their denomination is the most ancient."[1]

To the Baptists of Germany and Holland succeeded *the English and American Baptists*, now so actively and successfully diffusing their principles, and establishing their churches, in every quarter of the world.

Thus, briefly to recapitulate, we see that the Baptists may be traced from the ages immediately succeeding that of the Apostles and of those who received the gospel directly from their lips, through the Novatians, the Donatists, the Paulicians, the Paterines, the various communities of Waldenses, down to the Reformation, and thence through the so-called Anabaptists of Germany, the Mennonites or Dutch Baptists, the Baptists of England and those of this country, to the present time. Or, inverting the order, we may trace them from our

[1] Hist. Neth. Ref. Ch., Translation in S. Bap. Rev., April, 1859. See also Encyc. Rel. Knowl., Art. Mennonites.

own times to the Reformation, and thence through the various parties which we have named, up to those who "were first called Christians at Antioch."

We had not intended to notice the charge against the Baptists that they originated with the fanatics of Munster. It did not seem to deserve it. No person of intelligence and candor believes it. And we thought it would be no great exploit to demolish this "man of straw." The charge is sufficiently refuted by the proof which we have already furnished of their apostolic origin and character, and of their continued existence throughout all the Christian ages preceding the Reformation. And yet, inasmuch as that charge is so often brought by the uninformed and the prejudiced, in disparagement of the Baptists, it may, perhaps, be proper briefly to notice it.

The Baptists had been in being full fifteen hundred years when Bockhold, Matthias, and their frantic followers commenced their career of folly and of crime. "Munster was a German forest, where the Saxon savage chased the scarce wilder boar, when the master and his disciples laid the foundation of our history. The blood of that Cæsar who drove Ariovistus to the Danube, was not yet extinct in the veins of Nero, when Baptists were clustering among the hills of Rome. The fading light of letters and of art still played in lingering beauty on the marble slopes of the Acropolis, when hundreds of Athenian and Corinthian believers were buried with Christ in baptism."[1]

A brief comparison of the character and principles of the men of Munster, with those of the Baptists, would suffice to show that the latter could not possibly be the true descendants and successors of the former. Like produces like. Men do not gather grapes of thorns nor figs of thistles. A bitter fountain cannot send forth sweet waters. "The Munster Sect," says Dr. Brown, in his Life and Times of the great Baptist leader, Menno, "was a 'handful' of men resembling the modern Mormons. They claimed new revelations, not the Scriptures, as their guide in setting up their 'New Zion.' Their leaders were the successors of the 'Prophets of Zwickau,' in 1522. They had nothing in common with the Baptists, except the denial of infant baptism—for they held to a *worldly*, not a *spiritual* kingdom. At first, however, they were simple *enthusiasts;* persecution made them *fanatics.* 'Against the spirit, and word, and example of Christ,' says Menno, 'they drew *in their own defense* the sword, which Peter was commanded by his Lord to sheath.' We italicize the words 'in their own defense,' because the fact is commonly represented otherwise; and Menno's impartial testimony shows how much of the guilt and horror of

[1] Rev. J. Wheaton Smith.—Letter to Mr. Barnes.

the subsequent Munster tragedy, *is* really chargeable on the measures of the persecutors, who (before they drew the sword in self-defense) had long inflicted on them the most cruel immolations, butcheries, and murders. The fanatical proceedings at Munster, in 1534, under John Bockhold, the prophet, polygamist and bloody tyrant, shocked all men of common sense and decency; but none more than Menno."[1] "I warned every man," says he, "against the Munster abominations in regard to a king, to polygamy, to a worldly kingdom, to the sword, etc., most faithfully."[2]

After giving a full account of Menno, telling in his own words of his renunciation, as a Papist, of his "anti-Christian abominations, mass, infant baptism, loose and careless life, and all," and saying that "with a penitent heart he was 'buried with Christ by baptism,' and joined the martyr church of the New Testament—that church more ancient than Rome—opposed to all its corruptions, and persecuted in every age, because so pure, Dr. Brown adds—"It is now too late in the day to confound this primitive people with the 'Munster sect,' because both were called, by their enemies, 'Anabaptists.' As well confound the Baptists of the United States with the Mormons of Nauvoo.

[1] Life and Times of Menno, pp. 21, 22. [2] Ib. p. 23.

This is proof of pitiable ignorance. Learned Romanists knew better."[1]

One of those learned Romanists, not cited by Dr. Brown,—"a sincere Catholic," having "the reputation of a learned and liberal theologian," was, in 1564, employed by the Duke of Cleves to convert the Anabaptists. He had an intimate acquaintance with them and their history; and his testimony concerning them is introduced into Bayle's Dictionary, with these words: "No author has represented this sect with so much justice as George Cassander." Speaking of these so-called Anabaptists, Cassander says—"In which people you may in general discover marks of a certain pious disposition of mind; who, carried away by a zeal not according to knowledge, have erroneously, not maliciously, departed from the true sense of the inspired writings and the general consent of the whole church; which is evident from hence, in that they always strenuously opposed the rash attempts of those of Munster, who were contriving a new sort of establishment of the kingdom of Christ, which consisted in destroying the impious by external force; and have always taught that the establishment and propagation of Christ's kingdom depended solely upon the cross."[2]

[1] Life and Times of Menno, pp. 24, 25.

[2] Præfat. Tractat. de Baptismo Infantium, as quoted in Bayle's Hist. and Crit. Dict., Art. Anab.

The author of the Historical Inquiry into the Waldensian Origin of the Dutch Baptists, a recent able writer to whom we have already referred, alluding to the desire which an "extremely prejudiced Romanist writer" manifested to identify the Baptists with the fanatics of Munster, says that he "may be quoted as evidence, in spite of himself, of the different principles or different origin of the Baptists and Anabaptists."[1]

But really learned Protestants, as well as learned Romanists, "know better" than to confound the Baptists with the insurrectionists of Munster. D'Aubigne considers them "as different as possible." Guy de Bres, "a writer," as Bayle says, "who has exerted his whole force in refuting this sect," (the Anabaptists, or rather the Baptists,) and of whom he speaks as "an evidence which cannot be suspected," aids, indirectly at least, in their vindication. "He gives," says Bayle, "not the least hint that the Anabaptist martyrs, [the martyrs of the Baptists proper,] suffered death for taking up arms against the state, or stirring up the people to a rebellion."[2]

Very decided are the statements upon this subject, of the authors of the History of the Reformed Church of the Netherlands. We give a few of the more important of them. They affirm that the

[1] See Translation in So. Bap. Rev., Oct., 1857.
[2] Bayle's Hist. and Crit. Dict., Art. Anab.

"rebel Anabaptists," as they style them, "ought by no means to be considered the same as the Baptists"—that the insurrectionists "were people of every variety of religious belief, and many of them of no religion at all"—Catholics, Lutherans, Zuinglians, Anabaptists, properly so called, (those, as these authors define them, who "baptized all who passed over to their community, even if they had been baptized in another society at an adult age,")[1] and infidels—that they "made themselves notorious in the Netherlands for the most unheard-of seditions, in which were manifested a folly and *regardlessness of religion*, of a most surprising character"—that they "deserved the just hatred of all well-meaning persons, as *a herd of turbulent vagabonds* every where dreaded"—that "the Baptists generally, both by word and deed, testified that their peace-loving hearts abhorred the seditious conduct of the Anabaptists"—and "that

[1] "Anabaptists, a name which has been indiscriminately applied to Christians of very different principles and practices, though many of them object to the denomination, and hold nothing in common besides the opinion that baptism ought always to be performed by immersion, and not administered before the age of discretion. Anabaptists in a strict and proper sense, appear to be those who not only re-baptize when they arrive at an adult age, persons that were baptized in their infancy, but also as often as any person comes from one of their sects to another, or as often as any one is excluded from their communion, and again received into the bosom of the church, they baptize him."—*Encyc. Brit., Art. Anab.*

when the Anabaptists had taken Munster, the Landgrave of Hesse, a Lutheran, but inclined to the Baptists, furnished the Bishop with the munitions of war, that he might storm the city, and destroy the wicked rebels." After stating that partly through inability to make the proper discriminations, and partly on account of the prejudice under which they labored, in judging any thing which had reference to the Reformation, "the majority of the Romanists knew no difference between the various Protestant parties and sects, and would make no distinction," and that "the abhorrence only deserved by some of the Anabaptists, was bestowed upon all Protestants," the same authors say, "The honest Baptists suffered the most severely from this prejudice, because they were considered by the people to be the same, and were called by the same name. The fact that they agreed in their opinions respecting the holy ordinance of baptism, was the unfortunate occasion of this thing. On this account, the Baptists in Flanders and in Friesland suffered the most terrible persecutions." Blinded by their prejudices, their enemies "would not see that which they might have seen. How evident it was, that although the Baptists appeared to agree exactly with the Anabaptists in respect to the baptismal question, the former entirely disapproved of the course pursued by the latter. For it had been, and continued to be, a doctrine of the Baptists, that the bearing of arms was very unbecoming to a Christian. Did not the Anabaptists pursue a course directly the opposite of this? Did not all which they in their folly called religion, rest upon a most pernicious principle, which permitted the Christian, with fire and sword, to murder princes on their thrones? Among these people, were not all things made to yield to the demands of a licentiousness, the only tendency of which was to make the earth a howling wilderness, filled with men who would devour each other like wild beasts? Who could have imagined that such a purpose prevailed among the Baptists, who were the meekest of Christians? * * We have nowhere seen clearer evidences of the injurious influence of prejudice, nowhere have we met with a more obstinate unwillingness to be correctly informed; and a more evident disposition to silence those who better understood the truth of the matter. Prejudice, when once deeply imbibed, blinds the eye, perplexes the understanding, silences the instincts of the heart, and destroys the love of truth and rectitude. * * The Baptists are Protestant Christians, entirely different from the Anabaptists in character. They were descendants from the ancient Waldenses, whose teachings were evangelical and tolerably pure, and who were scattered by severe persecutions in various lands, and, long before the time of the

Reformation of the church, were existing in the Netherlands."[1]

Though we have already said much more than we had intended to say upon this subject, we cannot refrain, now that we are on it, from giving the testimony of another distinguished witness. The writer of the article on the Anabaptists in the Encyclopœdia Britannica, after stating that "it must be acknowledged that the true rise of the numerous insurrections" with which the name of the Anabaptists is connected, "ought not to be attributed to *religious opinions*;" that "the first insurgents groaned under the most grievous oppressions," and "took up arms principally in *defense of their civil liberties*;" that, of "the commotions that took place, the Anabaptist [not Baptist] leaders seem rather to have availed themselves, than to have been the prime movers;" that "it appears from history that a great part" of the insurgents "consisted of Roman Catholics, and a still greater of persons who had scarcely any religious principles at all;" and that "it appears reasonable to conclude that *a great majority of them* were not Anabaptists," goes on to say: "Before concluding this article, it must be remarked that the Baptists or Mennonites in England and Hol-

[1] Hist. Neth. Ref. Ch., Translation in S. Bap. Rev., April, 1859.

land are to be considered in a very different light from the enthusiasts we have been describing; and it appears equally uncandid and invidious to trace up their distinguishing tenet, as some of their adversaries have done, to those obnoxious characters, and then to stop, in order as it were to associate with it the ideas of turbulence and fanaticism, with which it certainly has no natural connection. Their coincidence with some of those oppressed and infatuated people in denying baptism to infants, is acknowledged by the Baptists; but they disavow the practice which the appellation of Anabaptists implies, and their doctrines seem referable to a more ancient and respectable origin. They appear supported by history in considering themselves as the descendants of the Waldenses, who were so grievously oppressed and persecuted by the despotic heads of the Roman hierarchy; and they profess an equal aversion to all principles of rebellion, on the one hand, and to all suggestions of fanaticism on the other."[1]

In reference to the absurd statement concerning the American Baptists, that they owe their origin to Roger Williams, and that his baptism being irregular and defective, they are without valid baptism, it is sufficient to state that he never baptized any one who baptized others, and that his irregu-

[1] Encyc. Brit., Art. Anabaptists.

lar baptism ceased with himself and the few private individuals whom he baptized. While the American Baptists, with a worthy pride in the character and achievements of the great champion of civil and religious liberty, are always ready to recognize him as a member of their community, they acknowledge no ecclesiastical dependence whatever upon him. They stand "upon the foundation of the apostles and prophets, Jesus Christ himself being the chief corner-stone."

We hesitate not to say, however, that if all the Baptists of this country were compelled to trace their baptism to Roger Williams, we should consider it far better than that of those by whom it is contemned. We should regard it as *real*, if *irregular*, while that of our opponents is neither regular nor irregular *baptism*. But even if it were, it would be no better than—nay, not so good as, that derived from Williams. He baptized, after having received the rite at the hands of a *Christian* layman. Those from whom they received it, obtained it, directly or indirectly, from the *antichristian* clergy of the apostate church of Rome. And even the poor authority, thence derived, was subsequently revoked with anathemas and bulls of excommunication.

IV.

PRINCIPLES OF THE BAPTISTS.

Baptists charged with Narrowness of Views—Deny the Charge—Appeal to the Infallible Standard—Views chiefly objected to—Calvinism—Theory of the Church—Baptism—The Lord's Supper.

IF, as we have shown, the Baptists derive their origin from Christ and his apostles, and are still essentially what they were in the beginning of their history, it follows that their principles are pure and scriptural, adapted eminently to honor God and to bless the world. That this is true of what are considered their more important principles, is, we believe, generally conceded. By common consent, they are ranked with the denominations of Christians generally esteemed strictly orthodox and evangelical. Yet, strangely enough, many who profess thus to esteem them, charge that they are, as compared with some of those denominations, remarkably contracted in their views and principles. To this indictment, as to others which we have noticed, the Baptists plead—not guilty. They regard the gospel as the broadest and most liberal system ever promulgated among men. And they believe undoubtingly, that their principles and those of the gospel are in all essential respects identical. If Christianity be contracted, then are they so; but if that be distinguished by a broad and sublime comprehensiveness, then are their principles marked by the same high characteristic.

They have no disposition to draw invidious comparisons between themselves and others, and would neither measure nor be measured by human standards. By the infallible standard of divine Truth, and that only, would they try and be tried. While sensible of many and great imperfections in their own individual character and conduct, and deeply deploring them, while confessing, with humiliation and sorrow, that they often fail practically to realize the true beauty and divine glory of their principles—yet believing, as we have said, that those principles are the principles of the gospel itself, and trusting that they love truth more than party, they are willing and even anxious that those who urge objections to them, should put them to the most thorough and searching evangelical tests.

The fairest and most satisfactory way, perhaps, of meeting the objection of narrowness brought against the principles of the Baptists, would be to state those principles in full. With the intelligent and candid, a distinct statement of them would be their best vindication. They shine with the pure, unborrowed light of heaven. They speak with the voice and authority of God. But we have not space for such a statement, with what else we have to say upon the charge under consideration. We must, therefore, content ourselves with a more limited view, confining it to those principles objected to by their opponents.

The Baptists are charged with narrowness in respect to their views of what are commonly called *the doctrines of grace.* Some of their opponents seem anxious to fix all the odium that may attach to an exaggerated and grossly misrepresented Calvinism upon the Baptists alone, or chiefly. But if there be such odium, let it be borne in mind that others share it with the Baptists; and that, so far as Calvinism is concerned, they are in what is generally considered good company. They stand not only with Calvin, but with the ablest and best of the Christian fathers—with Luther, with Knox, with Whitefield and Chalmers, Edwards and Dwight, with the Westminster Assembly of Divines, with the fathers of the church of England, as well as with innumerable others, good and great as they.

The views of the Baptists respecting the doctrines of grace, are either much misunderstood by many, or perversely misrepresented. Their so-called Calvinism is older than Calvin, older than Augustine, old as Christianity itself. If they hold to the doctrines of the sovereignty of God, predestination, election, and the final perseverance of the saints, it is not as many of their ignorant or prejudiced opponents represent them; it is as they are set forth by God himself. They hold them as Paul and the other inspired servants of Christ held them.

In connection with these doctrines, the Baptists are often charged with limiting the grace of God, and denying the universal freeness of the gospel. But they believe that God is no respecter of persons; that all, in every nation, who fear him and work righteousness, are accepted with him; that the gospel is without money and without price, and that whosoever will, may freely enjoy its benefits; that if any one perishes, it is because he will not come to Christ that he may have life. They believe, and teach, and preach, that "God so loved the world that he gave his only begotten Son, that whosoever believeth in him should not perish, but have everlasting life." If this be narrowness, then are the Baptists narrow.

Another ground of the charge of narrowness, respects their *theory of the church.* In what we shall have to say, in another section, upon the polity of the Baptists, we trust we shall be able to show that their theory of the constitution and government of the church is not justly amenable to this charge. We, for the present, limit what we have to say concerning it, to their views in respect to the *character* and *constituency of the church.*

They regard the church, in its highest and best sense, as inclusive of all the people of God, in every nation and in every age. They believe that while it is exclusive of many who have been, so far as the external act is concerned, rightly baptized, it is inclusive of all, whether so baptized or not, who truly love God, and honestly strive to know and do his will. But they do not believe it to be inclusive of the unregenerate, whether adults or infants, baptized or unbaptized. Its members are those only who have been "born, not of blood, nor of the will of the flesh, nor of the will of man, but of God." Of this church, not baptism, but Christ himself, is the door. And it is only through faith in him that any one can enter it. Those who seek admittance by any other way, will be forever excluded as intruders.

With respect to the church, in its literal and usual sense, as an outward and local organization, they believe that it regularly and rightly embraces all, whatever their age, position, or other outward circumstances, who, giving credible evidence of genuine piety, and personally professing faith in Christ, have been, in declaration of that faith, baptized into the name of the Father, the Son, and the Holy Ghost, and formally received into the company and fellowship of God's people. That it embraces infants, or others, whatever their age, position, or character, who do not fulfill the above-mentioned conditions, they do not believe.

It is to this latter view of the church especially, as narrow, that not a few take exceptions. Some maintain that the church visible is composed of all true believers and their infant children; and others that it is composed of all the baptized, whether adults or infants, the children of believers or of infidels.

In denying baptism and church-membership to infants, the Baptists are said to exhibit greater narrowness than the proverbially illiberal and exclusive Jews, who embraced infants as well as adults in their ecclesiastical system. To some of their opponents, indeed, the principle upon which these blessed privileges, as they are esteemed, are withheld from infants, seems so contracted as to have its source in nothing less than a want of the finer feelings of humanity, and to indicate a callousness and cold-blooded cruelty which are the reproach of our nature. To exclude tender babes from the church of Christ, weak and innocent lambs from the fold of the Good Shepherd, seems to them to re-enact the part of those who, when certain persons brought little children to Jesus that he might bless them, "forbade them;" and to deserve a severer rebuke than they received. It appears to them scarcely less than monstrous thus to treat the weakest, most helpless, and only innocent portion of the race. They often speak of it as consigning them, with pagans and infidels, to the "uncovenanted mercies of God," and sometimes even as consigning them to perdition. In expatiating upon this phase of Baptist exclusiveness and narrowness, their opponents often grow exceedingly touching and eloquent. But we regard all this expenditure of sentiment and eloquence as very unnecessary. He who, while on earth, took little children, without baptism, into his arms, clasped them to his bosom, blessed them, and said, "Of such is the kingdom of heaven," loves them still, and no less tenderly now that he is in the skies than when he was on the earth; and no less ready is he there to receive their spirits to his embrace, than he was here to receive their bodies.

This is a question of religious principle, rather than of natural feeling and human sympathy. And as such it should always be regarded.

Surely reason, enlightened and guided by the word of God, neither requires nor sanctions the baptism and formal introduction of infants into the church. Christianity is essentially a *voluntary* system. The reception of baptism and union with the church are, therefore, or should be, *voluntary acts.* But infants are incapable of any consciously voluntary act at all. They have not, therefore, the first and most necessary qualification for baptism and church membership. The unconscious babe knows nothing of the organization of which it is proposed to make it a member, and nothing of the act by which it is proposed to make it such.

Nor would the infant be able, by its baptism and reception into the church, to impart any spiritual benefit whatever to others, or to receive any from them. Its membership, therefore, would be at best only *nominal* and *honorary*, rather than active and real. But it is of the very genius of Christianity to deal in the real rather than in the ideal, in the substantial rather than in the formal. It is a system intensely practical. There is nothing ideal and sentimental, nominal and merely honorary about it.

What useful purpose could the membership of a child in a church possibly subserve? If it die in infancy without baptism, and outside of the pale of the visible church, no one but the Papist or the semi-Papist would have any doubt concerning its future and eternal blessedness. Certainly no Baptist would. On the other hand, none but the Papist or the semi-Papist believes that if it lived within the pale of the church to years of accountability, and then died without faith, its baptism in infancy, and membership in the church, would be of the least avail.

If it be suggested that the baptism and church-membership of the infant would make it more likely than if unbaptized and holding no such membership, to exercise, at the proper age, faith and repentance, it may be replied that facts do not at all justify any such inference. Is there any magic in mere membership in the church? Any marvelous, mysterious virtue in the waters of baptism? It has been truly said that "baptized children often grow up to be baptized infidels." If we mistake not, almost all the most noted infidels of modern times, Bolingbroke, Shaftesbury, Gibbon, Hume, Hobbes, Voltaire, Volney, Rousseau, were baptized infidels.

We doubt not that a careful collection and collation of statistics upon this subject, would show that the children of those who do not observe the rite of infant baptism, are at least as often and as early converted, as the children of those by whom it is most strictly observed. "In the city of Baltimore, it appears by the annual reports of the Sunday-school Superintendents' and Teachers' Association, that for several years the proportion of scholars professing religion, in the Baptist schools, was at least three times as great as in the Pedobaptist schools."[1]

The family, which is as much an institution of God as the church itself, is the proper place for the child—the true sphere in which to train it. Home influence is the great influence, as well for spiritual as for natural developement. If the child be neglected in the private sanctuary of home, it suffers a loss for which neither the public sanctuary of the church, nor any thing else can make amends. But is the home religious influence of the humble and truly devout Christian man who conscientiously rejects infant baptism as the invention of man, less than that of him who accepts it as of divine origin and authority? What is there in the rite, to make the latter more faithful to either his children or his God, than the former? Nothing! Surely nothing! unless to recur to the preposterous hypothesis already made, we find it in some mystic spell, some talismanic charm, about the baptism of an infant, which the parent feels, though the child be unconscious of its power. The Baptist as well as the Pedobaptist, loves his children. He, too, is a man, with all the feelings of a man—a parent with all the inextinguishable instincts of a parent. He desires for them above all earthly riches and honors, the

[1] See Rev. F. Wilson's Comp. Influence of Bap. and Pedobap. Principles in the Christian nurture of Children.

riches of truth, the honors of Heaven. He early instructs them in the word and will of God. He prays for them. He prays with them. He reads to them the Holy Scriptures. To stimulate their interest, he places the Holy Book in their young hands, and reverently listens to the word of truth as in soft, sweet, accents, they pronounce it. And as soon as their expanding minds are capable of deriving spiritual profit from them, with affectionate simplicity, he expounds to them its sublime and saving principles. He leads them to the house of God. That they may feel its healthful stimulus, and share in all its hallowed influences, he early introduces them into that nursery of the church, the Sunday-school. What other and more effective means can the most intelligent and pious Pedobaptist employ?

Not only does reason show *the futility* of infant baptism and church membership, it shows them to be *positively injurious.* Scarcely can any act, however trivial and simple, be entirely negative in its influence. If it do no good, it is sure to do harm. Such negativeness of influence, however, many have ascribed to infant baptism. They have said, "It is at least an *innocent ceremony,* and while we do not believe that it can benefit the recipient of it, we do not see how it can possibly injure it." But has God authorized the serious and religious performance in his name, of an act that has no significance, that is of no utility? Surely it does not become grave and reverend men solemnly to perform such an act, claiming for it divine significance, and enforcing it by divine sanctions. Such a rite, so performed, however unimportant in itself, claiming the authority of God, and purporting to be in fulfillment of the Saviour's parting injunction to his apostles, and which is supposed, in the language of many who perform it, to engraft the infant recipient of it into Christ, make it a child of God and an inheritor of the kingdom of Heaven, cannot be without vast influence.

If it do not affect the subject of it now, it will hereafter. It forestalls his inalienable right of personal choice. It fixes him in an involuntary and false position, from which in subsequent life, it is difficult to extricate himself. To say the least. it may greatly embarrass and distress him. But this is not all, nor the worst. Teaching him to regard himself as a member of God's church, identified with God's people, it may lead him to indulge a false hope, and to repose in a false and fatal security. And this, there is the greatest reason to fear, it often actually does.

It may, too, and doubtless does, exert a baleful influence upon the minds of parents, cultivating in them a superstitious trust in the saving efficacy of a mere outward rite. Hence it is that many a Pedobaptist parent, who feels his baptized and dying child to be secure, would have, if it were unbaptized, the most painful misgivings concerning its future fate.

Nor is the administrator of the rite himself unaffected by it. It burdens his mind with worse than worthless error ;—error noxious, and so far as its influence extends, destructive. More than this, it may involve him in the sin of both adding to and detracting from the gospel, and even, to some extent, in that of preaching "another gospel," and thus expose him to the fearful curses pronounced upon those sins.

Still further. It exerts a most deleterious influence upon others not immediately concerned in it —upon the whole Christian community—nay, upon the whole world. This is certainly its tendency, and this really its effect. It has in many instances subordinated the inward spiritual grace to the outward physical rite, and thus put the church and the so-called "sacraments" above Christ and the Cross. It has united in unholy wedlock, the church and the state—from which union has proceeded a brood of hybrid monsters devouring and desolating all that is fairest and best on the earth. It has confounded the just distinctions between the righteous and the wicked, the church and the world. It has degraded her who should have been the Bride, the Lamb's wife, into a harlot.

These evils, not to name others, reason—in the

light of scripture, experience, observation, and history—teaches are likely to result, as they have heretofore resulted, from that unscriptural breadth, which embraces within the church of Christ, those devoid of the essential qualifications for membership—the breadth which their opponents are so fond of bringing into uncharitable, and we fear invidious, contrast with the alleged narrowness of the Baptists.

But revelation, more authoritative than reason, neither requires nor sanctions the reception into the church of Christ of any who do not personally profess faith in Him. The narrowness which denies it, and of which the opponents of the Baptists so much complain, is the narrowness of the gospel itself. No precept, or precedent for the baptism and church-membership of infants, is any where to be found in the Holy Book.

Baptism is an ordinance of the New Testament. This the opponents of the Baptists admit. But if it be so, then the authority for its administration, must and can be found there. We need not involve ourselves in the mazes of Abrahamic covenants, and Mosaic institutes, in far-fetched, indeterminate inferences from this isolated passage of Scripture, of difficult interpretation and uncertain import, and that dark saying of some early father. No: *a positive institute* must be *positively instituted.* And if it be intended for *all classes* of persons, the unlearned as well as the learned, the weak as well as the strong, it should, one would think, be especially direct, and clear, and unequivocal, as well as positive.

But neither from the Abrahamic covenants, nor the institutes of Moses, more than from disputed passages of the holy or patristic writings, can the practice of infant baptism be sustained. This has been often and triumphantly shown in works widely read and accessible to all. Any formal reply, therefore, to the arguments on this point, of the opponents of the Baptists, even if our limits allowed, is here unnecessary. We will, however, take occasion to say, in passing, that the very length and difficulty of the argument from the Old Testament, for infant baptism and church-membership, furnish proof presumptive, very clear and strong, of the unsoundness of the theory which it assumes to defend—because it shows that instead of what we have every reason to require of its advocates, a *concise, clear, direct, positive* command, *from the New Testament,* they are only able to give us a *long, labored, involved,* and *difficult* argument, drawn from the Old Testament, and from a different and a *superseded dispensation.*

As we have said, our opponents admit that baptism is a New-Testament ordinance. We demand of them, therefore, New-Testament authority for its application to infants. They will never be able to furnish it. Men of learning and research, they have long made earnest and eager inquisition; but still has the object of their pursuit eluded them. After turning the sacred page by night and by day, not a few of them, with the learned German, Schleiermacher, have been constrained to confess that "he who finds infant baptism there, must first put it there."

We read of men and women being baptized, but of babes never. Nothing in favor of the baptism of infants but weak and far-fetched and strained inferences, at issue with the universally acknowledged principles of interpretation, as well as with the whole analogy of faith, are to be drawn from the accounts of household baptisms, as given in the New Testament. When fairly interpreted, all those accounts add greatly to the strength of the Baptist position. So, too, may we say with respect to the Commission; the famous passage already referred to, "Suffer little children to come unto me, etc.;" and that equally famous one, "Else were your children unclean."

No mention whatever of infants, in connection with baptism, is ever made in the New Testament. All the allusions to the members of the churches, as well as the manner in which they are directly addressed, show that they were adults, or at least not infants.

If infants were in the first churches, they were

most strangely and unaccountably ignored. If they formed so large a proportion of the membership of the early churches, if they engrossed so much of the official attention and ecclesiastical regard of the apostles, and those immediately following them, as upon the Pedobaptist theory it were reasonable to suppose, it is utterly unaccountable that during the whole apostolic age, and for a long period afterward, they were never named, nor even remotely alluded to as members. They are not now so ignored in Pedobaptist books, pulpits, prayers, papers, and pamphlets. The baptized children of the church are one of their commonest and most eloquent themes.

The charge against the Baptists of narrowness, is also warmly urged in connection with their views of *the act* of baptism. It is said that they exhibit great want of breadth and liberality in making that rite which it is affirmed is a mere application of water in the name of the Father, the Son, and the Holy Ghost, for the purpose of symbolizing spiritual purification, and the consecration of him who receives it to the service of God, essentially and necessarily an *immersion in water*—in making, as is alleged, the *quantity* of the water determine the validity of the rite—in making the *mere mode* in which the rite is performed, as important as, nay, more important than the rite itself—in subordinating the spirit to the form—in exalting baptism above other and more important requisitions of the gospel—in making it a saving ordinance, and in making a difference of views in respect to it—an unessential outward ceremony!—a cause of separation from their Christian brethren.

The Baptists regard baptism as something more than an emblem of purification and an act of consecration to God. It is inclusive of these, and of much more, which we have stated in another place. As to the question of much or little water, the Baptists regard it as altogether trivial, and not entering at all into the real issue between their opponents and themselves. Indeed they are entirely indifferent to the whole matter of mere water, however viewed, save in so far only as it furnishes the means of performing a most significant and sacred act. All they contend for is the *thing itself*—not the *means* nor the *modes* of its performance. Anciently the little river Jordan furnished waters as sufficient for the purposes of baptism, as those of the Mediterranean Sea. And the waters of the pool on the premises of the Jailor at Philippi, sufficed as well as those of the river Jordan. And so is it now. The Baptists of our day find it not less convenient to administer the ordinance in baptisteries than in rivers. It is their opponents—unlike the illustrious Harbinger of Christ, the great Baptist, having a horror of "much water" and a passion for little, as little as may adhere to a finger—who so stickle about *the quantity of water.*

Nor do the Baptists overlook the substance and true significance of the rite, in an exaggerated, unreasonable, and unscriptural estimate of the mere mode of its administration. While they are ready to admit that the mode of administering the ordinance of baptism, like the way of doing any other thing of serious import, is not without a certain importance, they yet consider the matter of *mere mode* of comparatively little moment. It is not, we repeat, for the manner of the act, but for the *act itself*, that they so strenuously contend. They insist that whatever the manipulations of the administrator, whatever the mode of administration, whatever the quantity of water applied, without immersion there is no real baptism. But whether the immersion be effected in *much* water or *little*, in a flowing stream or a standing pool, slowly or rapidly, gracefully or ungracefully, is wholly indifferent, so far as the validity of the baptism is concerned. As we said that it is their opponents, and not the Baptists, who make a question of the quantity of the water of baptism, so we say it is they, and not the Baptists, who make a question of *the mode* of baptism. It is they who clamor for mode—*the mode of sprinkling*, or *the mode of pouring*—advocating and defending it, in other ages, by fire and sword,—in our times, by tongue and pen, with all the powers of logic and of rhetoric, pathos and pleasantry, wit and ridicule, which they can command. If they really regard the mode so unimportant, why not for the sake of Christian charity, for the sake of the consciences of their weak Baptist brethren, for the sake of harmony and peace, for the sake of union and communion and the strength and happiness which they would give, for the sake of efficiency and success in winning souls, for the sake of the divine glory, why do they not adopt the *mode of immersion.* Ah! the opponents of the Baptists deceive themselves. The *mode* occupies an important place in their esteem. The *quantity of water* gives them great concern.

It is, too, our opponents who sacrifice the spirit to the form, in the administration of the rite, exalt it to an undue prominence as compared with other parts of the evangelic system, and endow it with magic power and saving efficacy. It is notorious that many of them, regarding with superstitious reverence the rite, attribute to it a strange, mysterious virtue, an incomprehensible and marvelous efficacy, nowhere accorded to it in the word of God. Including the Papists, the overwhelming majority, and excluding them, a very considerable proportion, of the opponents of the Baptists, regard it as *the act of regeneration*, a saving rite, without which the innocent and helpless babe is lost,—with which, the vilest criminal is saved.

On the other hand, the Baptists believe that all the baptismal waters of the world administered by the holiest of human hands, however they might wash away the filth of the flesh, would not suffice to take away the guilt of the soul. That for this high end, vain were the sacred floods of a thousand Jordans, vain the utmost potency of all the consecrated fonts of all earth's temples and cathedrals. That the blood of Jesus, and that alone, makes pure the polluted soul. That no one who has not already received that inward, spiritual cleansing, that baptism of the Holy Ghost which finds only its beautiful and striking emblem, in the outward rite, is prepared for the reception of that rite.

As to the charge of making a mere difference in respect to an outward and unessential ceremony, the cause of separation from their Christian brethren, it may be said that the Baptists do not regard any *ordinance* of God, in any proper sense, an unessential ceremony. They stand now, where they have always stood, with the truth of God—upon the same platform which was pressed by the feet of the Apostles and other early Christians. And it is not their fault, if their opponents are not with them. They have not caused the separation. The real controversy is not so much with them, as it is with the Bible Let their opponents cease to contend with that. Let them marshal themselves under the true standard. They will, we trust, by the grace of God, find the Baptists there. Their opponents parted company with them, when they parted company with the truth—when they substituted the traditions of men for the commandments of God. Let them come back to the truth. Let them cease by their traditions to make void the law of God—let them "inquire for the old paths, and walk therein," and they may again join company with the Baptists.

But the narrowness alleged against the Baptists is supposed most conspicuously to display itself in connection with their views of the *Lord's Supper*. And, singularly enough, this charge is generally brought by those who hold the very same principles in respect to the communion, by which the Baptists are governed.

The Lord's Supper is an ordinance commemorative of the sufferings and death of Christ on behalf of his people, and none have the right to participate in its celebration, who have not assumed, in baptism, the badge of discipleship. This is the outward sign by which Christ's people are distinguished; and no one without it, is, in strictness, any more to be regarded a member of the visible church of Christ, than he is to be regarded, without enrollment and the prescribed uniform, a member of the army. In these views, the Baptists agree with all other evangelical denominations, as might easily be shown by quotations from eminent authors among them all. As sufficient, however, for our present purpose, we here introduce the testimony of only two of them. The distinguished Dr. Griffin, President of Williams College, in his celebrated letter on Communion, says, "I agree with the advocates of close communion in two points: 1. That baptism is the initiating ordinance which introduces us into the visible church; of course where there is no baptism there are no visible churches: 2. That we ought not to commune with those who are not baptized, and of course are not church-members, even if we regard them as Christians. Should a pious Quaker so far depart from his principles as to wish to commune with me at the Lord's table, while yet he refused to be baptized, I could not receive him; because there is such a relationship established between the two ordinances that I have no right to separate them; in other words I have no right to send the sacred elements out of the church."[1]

Dr. Hibbard, perhaps the ablest writer on baptism and its kindred subjects, among the Methodists of this country, says: "It is but just to remark that, in one principle, the Baptist and Pedobaptist churches agree. They both agree in rejecting from communion at the table of the Lord, and in deny-

[1] See Bap. Lib. vol. iii. p. 211.

ing the rights of church fellowship to all who have not been baptized. Valid baptism they consider as essential to constitute visible church-membership. This also we hold. The only question, then, that here divides us, is, 'What is essential to valid baptism?' The Baptists, in passing the sweeping sentence of disfranchisement upon all other Christian churches, have only acted upon a principle held in common with all other Christian churches, viz., that baptism is essential to church-membership. They have denied our baptism, and, as unbaptized persons, we have been excluded from their table. That they err greatly in their views of Christian baptism, we of course believe. But according to their views of baptism, they certainly are consistent in restricting thus their communion. We would not be understood as passing judgment of approval upon their course; but we say, their views of baptism force them upon the ground of strict communion, and herein they act upon the same principles as other churches, *i. e.* they admit only those whom they deem baptized persons to the communion-table. Of course, they must be their own judges as to what baptism is. It is evident that, according to our views of baptism, we can admit them to our communion; but, with their views of baptism, it is equally evident they can never reciprocate the courtesy. And the charge of *close communion* is no more applicable to the

Baptists than to us, inasmuch as the question of church-fellowship with them is determined by as liberal principles as it is with any other Protestant churches, so far, I mean, as the present subject is concerned; *i. e.* it is determined by valid baptism."[1]

[1] Christian Baptism, pp. 174, 175; ed. 1845.

V.

SPIRIT OF THE BAPTISTS.

Illiberality and Exclusiveness of Spirit charged against the Baptists—Their History and present Attitude toward others Refute the Charge—Friends of every real "Evangelic Alliance"—Distinguished for Breadth and Expansiveness of Sympathy—Impossible for a true Baptist to be a Bigot—Persecuted but never Persecuting—Proselytism—Strict Communion.

THE Baptists are charged not only with narrowness of principle, but with illiberality and exclusiveness of spirit. It is said that they are so absorbed in devotion to their own party and its peculiarities, as greatly to neglect, if not in some instances entirely to overlook, principles vastly more important; that hence they are characterized by great want of Christian charity, and even by a spirit of intolerance.

That those views of the Baptists to which, as peculiar, exceptions are most generally taken, do not absorb an undue share of interest among them, and are not exalted into too great prominence, has been made apparent in what we have already said, and will yet further appear in what we have still to say. As to the charge that they are uncharitable and intolerant, we think their history, as well as their present attitude toward their Christian brethren of every name, furnishes a ready and complete refutation. Whilst honest, earnest, fearless, and ardent in the advocacy of their distinguishing tenets, and ready, rather than yield them, to suffer reproach and scorn, persecution and death, they have, in respect to all points of agreement, ever sympathized with others, and been ready in every feasible way to co-operate with them. This was strikingly shown at the Reformation. They differed widely in many important things from the leaders of that great movement; but, agreeing with them in others, they rose up in every part of Europe, and enthusiastically rallied to their support. And it was only when they discovered that the price of the distinguished alliance was the sacrifice of principles which they held dearer than life, and after having, for their devotion to them, been cruelly repulsed and persecuted, that they retired.

Another exemplification of the sympathy of the Baptists with others in every thing noble, is furnished by their course during the civil wars in England, in which the first Charles was dethroned and beheaded, and Cromwell raised to the supreme power. In vindication of what they esteemed the inalienable civil and religious rights of man, they united with those whose views, in all respects, they could not accept, and with them braved all the perils and shared all the sacrifices of those times. With them they sat side by side in the meeting for devotion; with them they knelt down in prayer; with them they stood shoulder to shoulder on the field of blood; and with them they lay down in death, martyrs for truth and freedom.

So, too, in our own Revolutionary struggle, the Baptists readily united with all who stood up for freedom.

Thus has it ever been. Thus is it now. In every movement, whose aim is the advancement of the cause of God and the promotion of the well-being of men, the Baptists, waiving their religious and denominational peculiarities, so far as it can be done without compromiting them, are ever ready to unite with any and with all others. They are ever among the fastest friends of every real "evangelical alliance." That great union of different denominations of Christians for the diffusion of the Holy Scriptures in all lands, the first organization of the kind, we believe, ever established, the British and Foreign Bible Society, owes its origin to Joseph Hughes, a Baptist. And to a Baptist deacon, the excellent William Fox, was due the organization of the first great national Society in England in behalf of Sunday-schools.[1]

No truer friends of the American Sunday School Union and the American Tract Society have there been than many of the Baptists. And if they now seem to show less interest in those, as well as in other kindred organizations, than formerly, it is only because they believe they can by separate action accomplish more for the cause of truth and righteousness on the earth, in similar institutions more directly under their own control, and now, in the incipiency of their existence, having special claims upon their sympathies and fostering care. They are still, however, as much friends to those national societies as other sects, each of which has its separate organizations.

For many years the Baptists were in close and zealous co-operation with the other leading evangelical denominations of the land in the American Bible Society. And it was only with the conviction that they could not be true to the claims of the truth of God, and the best interests of the world—a conviction forced upon them by what they esteemed, and still esteem, great inconsistency and injustice on the part of their associates, that they withdrew, and established an independent organization.

In those admirable institutions composed of young men of various Christian denominations,

[1] See Raikes and his Schools, p. 62.

now so generally existing in our cities, Baptists, in large proportion, are to be found. So, too, have they always been found in the union meetings for prayer, which have marked the progress of the recent great revival of religion. And this, too, although in some instances the most ill-timed and indelicate suggestions of measures calculated to compromise their principles, their self-respect, and their consciences, have been made.

The attendance of the Baptists, too, upon the ministry of others, whenever the just claims of their own allow, is a notable fact, and further corroborates the statement which we have made concerning the catholicity of their spirit. So, too, is the fact that they, more, perhaps, than any other religious community, are always ready to acknowledge and avail themselves of whatever is good in the writings of others. Scarcely among Pedobaptists themselves are to be found more appreciative readers of their ablest and best writings than among the Baptists. Conspicuous in the libraries of their ministers as well as private members, are to be found the standard expository and practical works of authors of every Christian name. And with a fearlessness and eagerness of inquiry, to which, we think, is found no parallel among others, are they always ready to examine even the most illiberal and bitter of the controversial productions of their opponents.

The *most individual, independent, and least clannish* of communities—proverbially popular in their sympathies—each one of them, when true to the principle and spirit of the brotherhood to which he belongs, may appropriate to himself the noble language of the Roman: "I am a man, and nothing that relates to humanity do I think indifferent to me." In all their social relations, in all their civil and ecclesiastical connections, they are distinguished for breadth and expansiveness of spirit rather than for narrowness.[1]

How grossly unjust, then, is the charge of a want of sympathy and brotherly love for others! Yet is it constantly made. Nor is this the worst. As we have said, we are even charged with *a spirit of bigoted* devotion to our peculiar views, and *intolerance* toward those of others. To this part of

[1] The following resolutions, passed at their late anniversaries by two Baptist State Conventions, illustrate the spirit of liberality to which we have referred as characteristic of the Baptists. The New Jersey Convention resolved: "That, while we, as Baptists, cannot yield our distinctive views conscientiously held, we cordially approve a large measure of *unity in spirit* and also of *unity in benevolent action* on common ground, among the different evangelical denominations." The New York Convention adopted the following: "That, while we can never sacrifice the principles which distinguish us as Baptists, we nevertheless hail with joy the increasing union of spirit among different denominations of Christians in the great work of saving men, and will most heartily and cheerfully co-operate with them in every work of faith and labor of love."

the charge we reply, that it were indeed one of the rarest of all rare things to find a whole community of men, or even a single individual, wholly free from the evil spirit of bigotry. Sure are we that those who so spiritedly charge it upon the Baptists, do in this very thing exhibit it themselves. The tone as well as the terms in which they bring the charge, were there no other, is evidence enough against them. And well, perhaps, were it, if, when it is said to them in the words of Jesus to the Pharisees, "Let him that is without sin among you cast the first stone," they showed as much sensitiveness and force of conscience as those displayed to whom the words were first addressed, when, without casting a stone, "they went out one by one."

It is fair to judge of the spirit of men by the principles which they hold, and the measures by which they seek to propagate them. Now, we have already shown that the principles of the Baptists are not justly chargeable with narrowness, but that they are broad and comprehensive as the gospel itself. If, then, the spirit determine the principles, in showing affinity for, and in adopting principles so wide and liberal as theirs, the Baptists demonstrate the breadth and liberality of their spirit. And if, on the other hand, the principles determine the spirit, then is there the same demonstration in their favor. In either case, it is established that the essential spirit of the Baptists cannot be narrow and intolerant. That there are individuals among them who may justly be charged with bigotry—nay, that some tincture of bigotry, because they are men, may attach to them as a community, we are by no means disposed to deny. But we insist that it attaches to them *as men* rather than *as Baptists.* No one, whatever may be his name or his professions, can be a bigot, without ceasing, in so far as he is a bigot, in that far to be a Baptist. And this we thus briefly demonstrate: The two prime articles of the Baptist creed are, 1. That the New Testament is the only and the all-sufficient rule of faith and practice. 2. That it is the inalienable right of every man to study and interpret that divine statute-book for himself. How, now, can a bigot be a true Baptist? No one will say that either the principle or the spirit of bigotry can be derived from the New Testament. And we have seen that the New Testament is the creed of the Baptists. Nor will any one say that he who acts upon the second great principle which we have named, can be a bigot. It is, then, impossible for a true Baptist to be a bigot.

But perhaps it is said that Baptists do not adhere to their principles, and are therefore bigots. Ah, that! Then our cause is gained. The principles and the true spirit of the Baptists are vindicated. All that remains is to vindicate them *as men*. But this we did not propose to do. We proposed to vindicate them *as Baptists*. As men, the Baptists are *like* all other men. As Baptists, they are very *unlike* them.

We have said we judge the spirit of an individual not only by his principles, but by the measures he pursues in practically carrying them out. How have the Baptists carried out their principles? In the spirit of them, we reply. They have never used the sword or the stake, the rack or the dungeon? They have never coerced any one. The only weapon they have ever wielded, even against their bitterest opponents, is that put into their hands by the Holy Spirit of God—the weapon of truth. They have never persecuted. It is sometimes said, sweepingly, that all sects persecute when they have the power. Alas! the Baptists too well know that it is *almost* true. They have felt the crushing power of Protestants as well as of Papists, of the Puritans of Old England and the Puritans of New England, of Lutherans and Calvinists, of Presbyterians, and Episcopalians, and Congregationalists. Yet the sweeping statement, to which we have alluded, is not *quite* true. One sect, of all the sects which have had the power to persecute, never used it—could not use it, without, in the act of seeking the destruction of its victim, aiming a deadlier blow at the organic law of its own being. It was the sect of the Baptists. Poor, persecuted people, downtrodden and despised, without a home, without a country, fugitives and wanderers, they were like their Lord, who had not where to lay his head. No crown ever begirt their temples, no robes of royalty ever invested their forms. Yet once it happened that a poor fugitive who had first fled to the wilderness from before the face of the "lord bishops" of England, and afterward to a second and drearier wilderness from the "lord brethren" of Massachusetts, in that wilderness set up a state, and established a civil government, which, in process of time became important. That fugitive was Roger Williams. That State was the Baptist State of Rhode Island, the first the world had known in which perfect freedom, civil and religious—"*soul liberty*," as Williams called it—was guaranteed to every citizen, and in which it was impossible to persecute.[1]

[1] It has frequently been asserted, especially within late years, that the Catholic founders of Maryland anticipated Roger Williams in the formal and legal establishment of religious liberty. But nothing were easier than to show that this is a very great mistake. The Lords Baltimore had very inadequate conceptions upon this subject, and never established complete religious freedom at all. They made, it is true, under circumstances which scarcely allowed them to do otherwise, some approximation toward it. But it was by no means, even under those circumstances, a very close approximation. The very enactments which professed to guarantee the free exercise of religion, de-

In connection with their alleged bigoted devotion to party and its peculiarities, is often brought against the Baptists the charge of a narrow and selfish spirit of *proselytism.* The only answer which the charge deserves is the *argumentum ad hominem.* It is doubtless often but the device of him who, having despoiled his neighbor of his goods, seeks by shouting at every step, "Stop thief!" to divert attention from himself.

There is a true and a false proselytism. The Baptists confess the former, but deny the latter. A truly aggressive church is the only church conformed in principle and spirit to the early churches, and to the gospel itself. But an aggressive church

nounced the severest penalties upon certain classes of religious offenders. Jews denying the Messiahship of Jesus, and Unitarians his Divinity, were liable to "death, with forfeiture of lands and goods." And all who, recoiling from the sin of Mariolatry, manifested a want of due respect for "the Blessed Virgin Mary," exposed themselves to "fine, whipping, and banishment." Subsequently, in the spirit of these enactments, and without violation of the original charter of the Colony, refusal to have one's children baptized was made in Maryland a heinous offense, and heavily fined. And, at a later day, the expression of certain religious opinions subjected the party guilty of it, not only to a heavy fine, but to the shocking and barbarous punishment of *having his tongue bored through.* Of the truth of these statements, both Bancroft and Hildreth, especially the latter, furnish abundant evidence. See, for a full and able discussion of this whole subject, Prof. H. H. Tucker's Letters to Hon. A. H. Stephens.

is a proselyting church. We would that the Baptists had more of the spirit of aggression upon error, and upon sin, more of a spirit of true proselytism. He who is in possession of the truth, is under the most sacred obligations to communicate it to others, and to strive in every lawful and honorable way, to induce them to accept it. This, Christ constantly taught both by precept and example,—"Freely ye have received, freely give." Having bountifully spread the banquet of truth, he commanded his servants to bid men come to it—to go out into the highways and hedges, and even compel the destitute and the starving to come.

But it is not more the duty of him who has the truth, to strive to win others to it, than it is to endeavor to convert them from error. The one, indeed, involves the other. And how blessed is he who zealously and faithfully performs a work so noble! "Brethren," says the Apostle James, "if any of you do err from the truth, and one convert him, let him know that he which converteth the sinner from the error of his way, shall save a soul from death, and shall hide a multitude of sins." "He that winneth souls is wise." And "they that be wise shall shine as the brightness of the firmament, and they that turn many to righteousness, as the stars for ever and ever."

The Apostles were famous proselyters. To convert men to their faith, they left no legitimate means untried. Paul, particularly, proselyted with wondrous boldness and success. He became all things to all men. To the Jews, he became as a Jew, that he might gain the Jews. To them that were under the law, as under the law, that he might gain them that were under the law. To them that were without law, as without law, that he might gain them that were without law. To the weak, he became as weak, that he might gain the weak.

The Reformers, too, were celebrated for their proselyting propensities. Luther was the very prince of proselyters. He drew over to his party more than fifty millions of the subjects of the Papal See. All the great modern missionaries, too, Carey, Marshman, Martyn, Morrison, Judson, and others, glowed with an intense and inextinguishable spirit of proselytism.

And we honor, most profoundly, all these proselyters. We praise their proselytism, as the highest exhibition of Christian virtue. It was not selfish and narrow-minded. It was disinterested and magnanimous. We commend the Christian for proselyting the Jew, the Mohammedan, the Pagan, and the Infidel. We commend the Protestant for proselyting the Papist. We commend all who have the truth, for proselyting to it those who are in error. We commend the Baptist, who, conscientiously believing that his Pedobaptist brother is in error, upon certain highly important points, strives by all honorable and scriptural means, to win him from it, to what he himself esteems the truth.

But the false and unscriptural proselytism to which we have alluded, is worthy of universal reprobation. How terribly was it denounced by Christ! "Woe unto you scribes and pharisees, hypocrites! for ye compass sea and land to make one proselyte; and when he is made, ye make him two-fold more the child of hell than yourselves." And how miserably is it now often exhibited, especially in cities, by many, who, like their prototypes of old, "love to go in long clothing."

The great scheme of proselytism is *the scheme of infant baptism.* There can be no doubt that an intense spirit of proselytism, as well as superstitious views of the rite, had much to do with its origin. "It was," says Benedict, "a strife and scramble to increase their party, and a spirit of rivalship among churches of different creeds, and not unfrequently of the same. Catechumens were hurried through their preparatory studies; the requisitions were continually diminished, until sponsors were admitted to make the needful answers for candidates for baptism, and then children of any age could be introduced to membership. And now, the great mass of Pedobaptist churches make their main dependence on their infant members for filling up their ranks. This peculiar kind of ecclesiastical adroitness enables them to have a constant supply in reserve. Those who join them from a conviction of the truth of their own sentiments, or on the profession of their own faith, would not be sufficient to keep their churches alive."[1]

Another plan of proselytism is that of the *union of church and state.* This, for ages, was the plan of all the opponents of the Baptists. To enhance their influence, and thus to increase the number as well as the weight of their adherents, they sought the power and patronage of the state. But to increase their worldly honor, to swell their numbers, or upon any other consideration whatever, never could the Baptists be induced to seek or to suffer such an alliance. On the contrary, they constantly and strenuously opposed it, even though thus their ranks might be thinned by desertion, or broken and scattered by persecution.

Still another mode of proselytism, is that of *a broad platform,—a latitudinarian creed.* And this, too, is the mode not of the Baptists, but of the opponents of the Baptists. The Baptists will not, as this very charge of narrowness now under consideration attests, either compromise their faith, or materially modify their practice, in order to increase their numbers. To do it, they will not substitute for baptism something that is not baptism, though

[1] Hist. Bap. p. 933.

thus, like their opponents, they might greatly enlarge their party. To gain favor with the world, though thus, too, they might strengthen themselves, in a mere human and earthly point of view, they will not violate the law and subvert the order of God's house, by admitting to the Eucharist the unbaptized. They will not receive into their churches along with the unbelieving, unregenerate, unbaptized, men of every theological cast and complexion.

These things being so, who, the Baptists or their opponents, are most obnoxious to the charge of a narrow and selfish proselytism?

We have said that the illiberality and exclusiveness of the Baptists, are thought to be especially shown in respect to baptism and the Lord's Supper. As we have, perhaps, in the preceding sections, said enough of *baptism,* and noticed all that is important in the charge of narrowness, whether of principle or of spirit, concerning that ordinance, we need say nothing further of it here. We shall, therefore, pass at once to a consideration of the charge as it relates to *the administration of the Eucharist.*

It is alleged that in not inviting to the Lord's table their brethren of Pedobaptist denominaions, the Baptists constitute themselves the judges of their consciences, discredit their religious profession, reject those whom God has accepted, and deny a place in the church below, to those who will be assigned a place in the church above. Now if these things were so, the Baptists would be indeed justly chargeable with the grossest illiberality and exclusiveness. They, however, deny the justice of these charges. They maintain that in witholding ceremonial communion from those whom they regard as unbaptized, it does not follow that they either make themselves their judges, impeach their whole Christian character, exclude them from their Christian sympathies, or deny them a place among God's people. And this, we think, we shall make apparent to every intelligent and candid mind.

The Lord's Supper is an ordinance purely *commemorative.* It is designed to be a remembrancer of Christ, outwardly simple and unimposing, yet beautiful and touching, to those for whom he offered up his life. None, then, but his people, can rightly celebrate it. And since it is an *outward and formal rite,* none even of these, but such as have made an open and formal declaration of faith in him. The mode *appointed by Christ, and universally observed by the primitive disciples,* of making such declaration, was *submission to baptism, administered in his name.* This is evident from the commission under which the gospel is preached, and all its ordinances administered. It requires that by preaching and teaching disciples be made; that they be then, in declaration of their discipleship, baptized; and that they be subsequently taught to observe all things whatsoever Christ has commanded. Among the things commanded by him, and to which in the commission he referred, was the commemoration of his death. And whatever the place of this one of those things, with respect to the others thus *generally* alluded to, it is obvious that it was designed to follow baptism, *previously*, as well as so *particularly, mentioned, and so prominently put forward.*

Nothing, in the way of precept or example, in the slightest degree favoring the notion that any but *baptized believers, in union and fellowship with the church*, ever participated in the sacred feast, is to be found in the New Testament. So clear and undeniable is this, that the scriptural precedence of baptism to the Lord's Supper, has been conceded in all ages, and by Christians of every class.

In proof of this statement, testimony the fullest and most satisfactory, could easily be adduced from the standards of all Christian denominations, as well as from eminent writers both ancient and modern, such as Justin Martyr, Jerome, Austin, Bede, Theophylact, Bonaventure, Spanheim, Lord Chancellor King, Dr. Wall, Wesley, Watson, Doddridge, Dwight—to name no more. As we previously saw, Robert Hall, the great champion of open communion, while strenuously contending that there is no necessary precedence of baptism to the Lord's Supper, yet admits, that in apostolic usage there always was such precedence. And he even goes so far as to say that if any one, in apostolic times, had insisted upon receiving the communion, while refusing to be baptized, he would have been repelled as a contumacious schismatic.[1]

The proper precedence of baptism to the Lord's Supper, is also sustained by *the very nature and relations to each other of the ordinances themselves.* Baptism, while symbolical of the burial of the natural, is symbolical of the birth of the spiritual man, the commencement of the new and divine life. The Lord's Supper is symbolical of the continued sustenance of that life. The one symbolizes that spiritual and divine process by which we are made new creatures in Christ Jesus—the other that by which we are constantly nourished and sustained by him, until, from being babes, we reach the stature of perfect men. The one, therefore, has been appropriately styled *the symbol of regeneration*, the other *the symbol of nutrition.* "In submitting to baptism," says the venerable Abraham Booth, "we have an emblem of our union and communion with Jesus Christ, as our great Representative, in his death, burial, and resurrection: and as in baptism we profess to have renewed spiritual life, so in communicating at the Lord's table, we have the em-

[1] Hall's Works, vol. i. p. 311.

blems of that heavenly food by which we live, by which we grow, and by virtue of which we hope to live forever. Hence theological writers have often called baptism the sacrament of regeneration or of initiation, and the Lord's Supper the sacrament of nutrition."[1] Dr. Dagg, having in view the passage just quoted from Booth, remarks,—"Baptism which is administered but once, denotes regeneration or the beginning of the new life. The Lord's Supper which is often repeated, denotes the nutrition of the regenerate, or the continued feeding on Christ by faith. It is, therefore, fit that baptism should be received at the beginning of the Christian profession, before any participation of the Supper." And, again,—"If regeneration precedes the life of faith; if we die with Christ, and rise to newness of life before we habitually receive by faith the benefits of his sacrifice, baptism ought to precede the Lord's Supper, or the natural order becomes inverted."[2]

The priority of baptism to the Lord's Supper, thus shown by the nature and relation to each other of the ordinances, as well as by the places assigned them in the Holy Scriptures, is also enforced by *practical considerations* of the very highest importance. The proper outward evidence of discipleship, is baptism and union with the church

[1] See Dagg's Essay on Strict Communion, pp. 12, 13.
[2] Ib. pp. 55, 57.

How else shall one be recognized as a follower of Jesus, and a friend of his people. We cannot read the heart. Shall we receive into our fellowship, and make ourselves responsible for any and every isolated individual who may simply in word, and perhaps from improper motives, profess faith in Christ and love for his people, while persistently disregarding the solemn commandment of the former, and habitually standing aloof from the society of the latter? Surely not. We rightly require that he shall give the proof of his loyalty to Christ by obedience to his commandment, in putting him on in baptism, and of his love for his people, by formally and openly seeking a permanent connection with them.

So far, indeed, from receiving into fellowship those who make no pretension to "walking in all the ordinances and commandments of the Lord blameless," the churches are solemnly charged to withdraw from those already in connection with them, whose walk is disorderly.—"Now we command you, brethren, in the name of the Lord Jesus Christ, that ye withdraw yourselves from every brother that walketh disorderly, and not after the tradition which ye received of us."—2. Thes. iii: 6.

Thus we see, both from Scripture, and the natural order of things, the proper and necessary priority of baptism to the Lord's Supper. We have also seen that in respect to that priority, we agree with our brethren of all Christian denominations. With what consistency, then, do they bring against us, for practically insisting upon it, the grave charges which we are now repelling? Why are they not only so unjust, but so inconsistent, as to charge as a fault in the Baptists, that which they regard as a virtue in themselves? Is their conscience sacred, and does ours deserve no regard? Are they to be commended for maintaining what they esteem the order and honor of God's house, and we to be reproached for doing the same thing?

The real issue between the Baptists and their Pedobaptist opponents, respects baptism rather than the Lord's Supper. And this—though some with reckless partisan unfairness, and others with exceeding illogicality, have often overlooked and ignored it—many, as we have seen, with a candor and magnanimity which do them the highest honor, fully concede. That in this issue, the argument is on the Baptist side, has been already, in other connections, briefly shown, and might, did our limits allow, easily be demonstrated at greater length.

It is clear, however, that even if the Baptists were in error upon the subject of baptism, they would not be chargeable with illiberality and exclusiveness. In common with others, they believe that only the baptized are entitled to a place at the Lord's table.

And they believe that only such as have been *immersed, upon a personal profession of faith*, are baptized. Hence they cannot without gross inconsistency, as well as moral guilt, invite to the table of the Lord, any, however pious and exemplary, who have not, upon such profession, been immersed. Were they to do so, they would be unworthy communion with their Pedobaptist brethren, and we do not see how the latter could honorably extend it to them.

The only way in which at all plausibly the course of the Baptists can be objected to, is to insist, as Dr. Griffin did, that they believe wrongly. But, as we have intimated, the Baptists could not, if they would, believe otherwise than they do. And the more they examine the whole subject in debate, the more they think, speak, read, write upon it, the stronger grows their faith in the correctness of their views. And did they not know something of the strength and inveteracy of prejudice, the force of early education, and the almost invincible power of social and ecclesiastical connections, it would seem to them utterly unaccountable that their brethren of other denominations, intelligent and pious as many of them unquestionably are, can so tenaciously cling to their present opinions. And they cannot but think that all they need in order to relinquish them, is freedom from the influences to which we have referred.

Not less liberal, in their *theory* of Communion, than others, the Baptists are not less so in their *practice* of it. None of the Pedobaptist denominations, when really consistent and true to their standards, will admit to the Eucharist those whom they regard as unbaptized. Exceptions to this rule, on the part of individuals and societies among them, there may be, but as denominations they are all agreed. The Quaker, having, as he supposes, received the higher and better baptism of the Spirit, rejects, as unnecessary, the baptism of water. His Pedobaptist brethren, acknowledging his piety, but not accepting his theological views, think themselves justifiable in refusing him a place at the table of the Lord. "Romanists," says a recent writer, "in certain cases of discipline and penance, to prevent scandal, and save appearances, will allow a prince or any other individual, where the motive is sufficient, to approach the altar and receive a wafer, but a wafer not consecrated, and therefore without virtue, which has been called a *blank, or white communion.*" A similarly *blank*, or *white communion*, the late venerable Bishop Moore of the Episcopal church in Virginia, once granted to a Quaker friend. "In the earlier part of his ministry, while officiating in the State of New York, on a certain sacramental occasion, he presented to the members of other denominations an urgent appeal inviting them to participate in the privilege of commemorating the dying love of Christ at his table. In this address he adverted to the right of Christians to commune together, representing it as the Lord's table, and denying the propriety of repulsing any of the Lord's people. The appeal had its desired effect. Several of different denominations came forward. Among others, to the surprise of Mr. Moore, was a prominent member of the Quaker persuasion, a man of highly respectable character, and of undoubted piety. The minister supposed that he might have changed his sentiments, and have been baptized. He approached the applicant as he knelt at the chancel, and affectionately inquired if he had obeyed Christ in baptism. He was informed that a change of sentiment had taken place with respect to the perpetual obligation of the Lord's Supper, but not in relation to the other ordinance. In this painful dilemma, Mr. Moore stated that for a moment he scarcely knew what was best to be done. He, however, soon determined that he could not conscientiously administer the communion to his Quaker brother, although he believed him to be a man of God, because he had not been baptized. He stated his difficulties to his friend, and requested him to retain his place, and he would simply pass him by in the administration of the elements."[1]

[1] See Taylor's Restricted Communion, p. 24.

But even *blank* or *white communion* is not always accorded the Quaker. "An intimate friend," says Dr. Dagg, "of my early days, who had been educated a Quaker, soon after having obtained a hope in Christ, happened to be present at a Presbyterian sacramental meeting, and was moved to request that he might be admitted to the table. He was refused, on the ground that he had not been baptized."

A prominent minister of the Methodist Episcopal church, a few years since, even while highly eulogizing Robert Hall, and expressing great admiration of his views on communion, admitted to the writer, that he could not conscientiously, and in conformity with the standards of his church, admit a Quaker, however pious, to the Communion.

Here we have Episcopalians, Presbyterians, Methodists, and, as we saw in a quotation from Dr. Griffin, Congregationalists also, agreed in excluding the unbaptized but pious Quaker from the table of the Lord.

But not only do Pedobaptists exclude Quakers from their communion, they often exclude each other. A few years since, the members of the Old School Presbyterian General Assembly refused a request for inter-communion, formally preferred by members of the New School General Assembly, then in session in the same place. The Episcopalian, in his own church, will commune with the Presbyterian, but he will not reciprocate the compliment, by receiving the sacred elements in the Presbyterian church, from what he regards as "unconsecrated hands." The several Scotch Presbyterian churches, the Associate, the Associate Reformed, the Reformed Presbyterian, or Covenanters, and the United Presbyterian, refuse to commune with any sect.

Thus we see that there is no such thing as the much-vaunted open communion, among Pedobaptist denominations. They are as close as Baptists —though with not half their consistency. Nay, they are closer than Baptists. To crown their closeness and their inconsistency, all these denominations refuse the communion to a large portion of their own membership. They will administer the rite of baptism, taking, as they suppose, the place of circumcision, to infants—but they will not administer the Lord's Supper, taking the place, as they equally believe, of the Passover, to these same infants. In the preceding section, we saw that it was considered exceedingly narrow in the Baptists to refuse baptism to children. Is it less so in Pedobaptists, after baptizing them, to deny them the Lord's Supper?

Surely the opponents of the Baptists are not so liberal in their views and sympathies, their principles and practices, as would become those who arraign others upon the charge of narrowness. It seems that a fair comparison between them and those whom they so freely censure, and so summarily condemn, would by no means enhance their credit for either breadth of view or liberality of sentiment. We have seen that they, for the most part, agree with the Baptists that immersion is true and valid baptism. They could, therefore, without any sacrifice of conscience, and with very little real inconvenience, certainly not more than that which the Baptists esteem it a privilege and an honor to encounter, adopt immersion universally as the act of baptism. Thus easily could they do much towards putting an end to the baptismal strife; thus easily could they restore one of the breaches in the walls of Zion—thus easily could they effect something of that union which they profess so ardently to desire. And yet they will not! Alas, for human consistency! Alas, for the eye that beholds the mote in another, but descries not the beam by which its own vision is blurred! Alas, for the heart that deeply repenting of the sins of another, so exhausts itself as to have no sorrow left for its own!

On the other hand, it cannot be said that the Baptists could just as easily adopt sprinkling or pouring for baptism. No! For in the light in which it appears to them, they could not do it without committing a *violent outrage upon their understanding.* It seems to them nothing less than the most unmitigated and preposterous solecism, to use no harsher term, to say—baptism *by sprinkling!* In their view it is tantamount to saying ing—immersion *by sprinkling!* But this is not all, nor the worst. To adopt sprinkling or pouring for baptism, they would have to commit the most *flagrant outrage upon their moral sense,*—they would have to stifle the voice of conscience. They believe it to be their duty, in obedience to the command of Christ, *to immerse,* not to sprinkle. To do the latter, then, for the former, would be, with their present views, the most unconscionable trifling with sacred things.

Further still. The gospel, in its purity, integrity, completeness, beauty, strength, divinity, is the greatest gift of God to man. Now, to corrupt this purity, to disturb this integrity, to lessen this completeness, to mar this beauty, to weaken this strength, to obscure this divinity, in any degree, is to wrong those to whom have been sent the glad tidings of great joy. And this is done by any perversion of the truth of the gospel, by any mal-administration of its ordinances.

But to outrage one's own understanding, and even one's own conscience, are yet lighter things than to *outrage the authority of God.* Presumptuously to do, as by authority of heaven, what he has not enjoined; rebelliously to leave undone, what he has commanded to be done! This great guilt the Baptists would incur, if, to win the approbation of others, they disregarded their conscientious convictions concerning any ordinance of God. Surely it is strange, passing strange, that professed Christian people, boasting that charity which rejoiceth not in iniquity, but only in the truth, should, in the name of truth and charity, demand it of them. This, however, they virtually do, when they insist that the Baptists shall admit to the Lord's table those who have not been immersed upon profession of faith in Christ. Hence it has happened, that when, in any case, yielding to the seductions of a spurious charity, they have thus compromised their principles, there have not been wanting, among their opponents, some to make it the occasion of taunting them with insincerity in their professions concerning baptism. "By adopting the plan of open communion," says the author of Modern Immersion not Christian Baptism, "they practically concede the validity of our baptism, as respects both the mode and the subject. As they profess to act only from plain examples or apostolic precepts, and as they can find neither in the New Testament for receiving persons at the Lord's table after Christian baptism was instituted, who, in the judgment of the first Christians were not baptized, we must take it for granted, notwithstanding all their evasions on this subject, that they consider Pedobaptists really baptized."

We cannot but think that many of the more intelligent and candid opponents of the Baptists misapprehend, in some important respects, the nature and design of the Eucharist, as well as the views of the Baptists in regard to it. They seem to consider the Lord's Supper, which is, in its primary design, a commemorative, and only a *commemorative rite*, as essentially a symbol of *universal spiritual communion among Christians*. But nowhere in the New Testament do we find it stated or in any way intimated that it was ever celebrated by *individual believers*, or by *general companies of Christians*, simply *as such*, and independently of *church relations*. The communion of the body and blood of Christ is "the joint participation" of his people, in communion with God,—communion with Him who died, with the Father who gave him to die, and with the Holy Spirit through whom are made available the benefits of his death.

Not only do many thus wrongly regard the Lord's Supper as the symbol of general spiritual communion between believers, but they make it *the one great symbol*, the *highest test* of such communion. The Baptists, on the contrary, do not believe that it was designed to be, even in the individual church which celebrates it, the highest test, or, indeed, any special test at all of *spiritual*

14

communion among its members. Such communion, in a very high degree, is often enjoyed; but it results incidentally, and is essentially such as is enjoyed in prayer and praise, and other acts of devotion. So far as it is a symbol at all, of communion between believers, the Lord's Supper is a symbol of purely and strictly *ceremonial* communion between them, *as members of the same individual church.*

Hence it appears that in maintaining their views and practice respecting this ordinance, Baptists do not arrogate to themselves peculiar sanctity, or any spiritual superiority whatever. They only claim for themselves greater *outward regularity*, a stricter formal and ceremonial conformity to the requisitions of the gospel, a fuller and completer obedience to the law of Christ than others exhibit.

Another erroneous view of the Lord's Supper, one which, doubtless, produces much of the sensitiveness manifested by many concerning it, and thus leads to the charge of illiberality and exclusiveness urged against the Baptists, is, that it is *holier*, and *more sacred*, than any other ordinance. God forbid that the Baptists should, in any degree, seem to detract from the beautiful and blessed ordinance commemorative of their dying Lord, and of the Love whose height, and depth, and length, and breadth, neither man nor angel may measure. But while according to it the utmost sacredness, while regarding it, like every thing that emanates from God, holy even as he is holy, they do not see wherein it is holier or more sacred than any other divine ordinance—than baptism, of which many sometimes speak so slightingly, and which, in instances not a few, they even seem to ridicule. The Eucharist may, indeed, suggest associations more impressive, more touching, more tender, to our human hearts, and therefore be invested by our feelings with greater solemnity and sacredness; but it is not intrinsically at all more important than some others; not really holier or more sacred than the least of them all.

Another error is that of supposing that open and universal communion would accomplish great good in promoting charity, union, and co-operation among the people of God. Facts by no means sustain this supposition. Are the intercommuning denominations more united than the non-intercommuning? Are Presbyterians and Methodists more affectionate towards each other than Presbyterians and Baptists? If so, is it brought about by free communion among them? We think not. The fact is that there is nothing in the nature of mere ceremonial communion peculiarly adapted to produce such union and co-operation. Practically, open communion is a nullity. It is a mere theory. Pedobaptists while extolling it, rarely practice it.

So far from unrestricted communion having a good effect, it would have, if universally practiced, a most deleterious influence. Its constant tendency is to a compromise of principle, to laxity of discipline, latitudinarianism of doctrine, and to a consequent lowering of the standard of individual piety, and of the character and efficiency of the churches.

It is well known that other denominations hold doctrines, and in some instances tolerate courses of conduct in their members, which are not held and tolerated by Baptists. Now how could the latter reasonably receive persons to their communion, who, if they were actual members of their churches, would be expelled for entertaining and advocating what they deem unscriptural and pernicious doctrines, and for practices esteemed by them incompatible with the Christian character? Such a doctrine is that of infant baptism, held by all the Pedobaptist denominations. Such practices are those of frequenting theatres, ball-rooms, and other places of worldly and sinful amusement, allowed by several of them. Well says the late venerable Dr. Cone, "In extending the right hand of fellowship, a church must be satisfied that the individual soliciting admission has scriptural views of himself, and of God, and of the way of salvation by Christ alone, and of the work of the Spirit, and of the holy tendency of divine truth; and hence we are directed to *mark* and *avoid those* whose erroneous sentiments cause divisions and offenses contrary to the *doctrine which we have learned.*—Rom. xvi. Moreover, the candidate for church communion must not only *converse* about the things of God in a proper manner, but his deportment must correspond with his holy profession. 'If any man that is called a brother, be a fornicator, or covetous, or an idolater, or a railer, or a drunkard, or an extortioner, we must not keep company with such an one, no, not to eat,' (1 Cor. v. 11); and *that course of conduct* which cuts off from the church one who is already a member, must be, by parity of reasoning, an insurmountable obstacle against admission to its privileges."

A striking illustration of the evil effects, practically, of admitting to the sacramental communion of the church, those who are not formally in fellowship with it, is furnished in the following, stated by Prof. Harvey as a "well-authenticated fact," in his recent essay on Communion: "A devoted and conscientious deacon of a Congregational church commenced to labor with a member of the same church for unchristian-like conduct, but could obtain no satisfaction. He then took one or two brethren with him, and spread out all the circumstances before them; but the man still justified himself. The church was at last compelled to exclude the offender. He then went to a neighboring

Methodist church, represented himself as persecuted because he had honestly changed his sentiments, and was cordially received. The next communion season which this Congregational church enjoyed, (or would have enjoyed but for mixed communion,) he came forward, and with great care takes his seat by the side of the deacon who took up the labor with him, for the express purpose of aggravating his feelings. The good deacon says to a member of the Baptist church present, (with whom he was very intimate,) 'Brother, what shall I do? I do not feel as though I could commune with that man? The Baptist replied: 'I pity you, deacon, from the bottom of my heart, but I cannot relieve you: this is the effect of your wrong view of communion.' The church was thrown into such a state of perturbation as to disqualify them to receive so holy an ordinance with pleasure or profit."[1]

We have said that many of the opponents of the Baptists misapprehend not only the true nature and design of the Lord's Supper, but also the views and feelings of the Baptists respecting it. They do so, especially, in supposing that the Baptists by refusing ceremonially to commune with those whom they regard as unbaptized, make themselves the judges of their consciences. One of the leading principles of the Baptists is that of the right of

[1] Terms of Communion, pp. 33, 34.

private judgment—a principle for which they have contended in all ages, and under all circumstances, in the loss of all things, and unto death; while many others were striving to banish it from the earth. Their opponents judge for themselves in receiving into their churches, in their own way, all applicants. This the Baptists do, and nothing more. They judge for themselves alone, and not for others.

Another misapprehension, on the part of their Pedobaptist brethren, is, that in refusing to commune with them at the Lord's table, they deny the genuineness of their piety. But this one fact alone is sufficient to show the contrary, viz., that believing all to be pious *before* they can rightly receive baptism, Baptists refuse to administer the sacred rite to any who do not give evidence of having become new creatures in Christ Jesus and entered into a state of salvation. It many a time happens that they refuse a place at the Lord's table, for the time, and upon principle, to recent converts whom they have already received as candidates for baptism. Will any one be so preposterous as to affirm that they deny their Christian character, and withhold from them all Christian fellowship and communion, when they have already indorsed and accepted them as true believers? Surely not. The case is similar with respect to their Pedobaptist brethren. Their position is the same as that of the young converts alluded to. They are recognized as believers, but believers yet unbaptized. And as *outward church-fellowship* and *sacramental communion* are denied the former, so are they denied the latter, and upon precisely the same principle.

All the fervid eloquence, therefore, which has been expended upon the enormous illiberality and exclusiveness of the Baptists, in refusing to commune on earth with those with whom they expect to commune in Heaven, has had no proper excitant, and been expended uselessly.

And now, in view of all that we have said, we confidently submit our cause to the candid and just of all parties, believing that they will acquit us of the charge of illiberality and narrowness.

So far, indeed, from deserving reproach, we think the Baptists deserve the highest honor for what is styled their *close communion*—terms which, as usually applied, should be, in common justice, disused, implying, as they do, that the Baptists are narrow and exclusive in their principle and practice of communion, while, in fact, as we have so fully shown, they are as wide and liberal as any others—nay, as the Gospel itself.

Baptists regard themselves as, in their sphere—their true and proper sphere, not beyond it,—custodians of God's truth, and guardians of the honor of his house. And while they do not at all claim the right to interfere with the administration of the Lord's Supper, as practiced by others, under such conditions as they conscientiously esteem to be right, they think that in all candor and charity they should not be upbraided and charged with illiberality for admitting among themselves applicants for the sacred rite, upon such principles, and under such conditions only, as they believe to have the warrant of the word of God. They claim for themselves only the same privilege of private judgment and the same rights of conscience, which they now, as they have ever done, freely accord to others. Surely there is no illiberality, no bigotry, in this! If there be, then we beg God, in his goodness, to give us more and yet more of it, and not only us, but others, all—and especially those by whom we are so unjustly and unkindly reproached.

If, as the Baptists have so often said, the Lord's table were *their table* only, then they might follow their mere natural and human, social and civil sympathies, as they do at their own boards and domestic hearths, and admit others to it. But because it is the Lord's table, and not theirs, they dare do so only upon the terms which their Lord has prescribed.

We believe that in their scriptural strictness of communion, modern Baptists have a most important mission to fulfill. It is to keep pure the ordinances of God's house—to lift up and keep on high the standard of their glorious Leader and their Lord; and thus, while vindicating their claim to be his true followers, to illustrate their spiritual and ecclesiastical connection with those noble witnesses for the testimony of Jesus, whose bones

> "Lie scattered on the Alpine mountains cold,
> E'en them who kept God's truth so pure of old,"

as well as with all who, in every age and every land, have, like them, "kept the faith."

VI.

POLITY OF THE BAPTISTS.

Objections to the Polity of the Baptists—Erroneous Views of the Church—Baptist Views—The Church both a Theocracy and a Democracy—Baptist System not more Radical than the Gospel itself—Not Agrarian—Not Inefficient—Admirably adapted to secure the highest Development of the Individual Believer and the utmost Efficiency of the Churches.

IT is objected to the Baptists that their church polity is too *democratic*; that it is *radical* and *agrarian* in its tendencies, deficient in *disciplinary power*, and wanting, generally, in strength and efficiency; that it gives to the uneducated and the ignorant as much authority and influence as to the most highly cultivated and refined; that, allowing no great, controlling, centralizing power, strifes and divisions weakening and rending the societies which adopt it are likely to be constantly engendered among them; and that, providing for no fixed organic union of all these societies, it furnishes no adequate means of making so imposing and effective a demonstration before the world, as is necessary widely, powerfully, and permanently to impress it.

In other ages, Baptist views of the constitution and government of the church called forth the severest denunciations. Their enemies not only insisted upon a prelatic authority, which the Baptists could not allow, but, with fiery zeal, upon an ecclesiastical unity and catholicity, in which the Baptists had no faith. Contending for unity as though it were a mere mechanical thing, they compelled it by external pressure, and thus secured an outward uniformity, while there was no oneness of mind and heart. These erroneous notions, with the unreasonable, unscriptural, and oppressive measures which were adopted to enforce them, the Baptists always resisted. They contended that true unity is the unity of the spirit—the unity of the spirit in the bonds of peace; not unity enforced by discord and contention; not unity produced by bonds of fear and of force. Hence, while always insisting upon spiritual and doctrinal unity, while uncompromisingly maintaining that there is but one Lord, one Faith, one Baptism; while fervently praying and assiduously striving for harmony of purpose and concert of action, they did not require any formal and inseparable confederation of their churches. The advocates of the false unity we have named, regarding it as of prime importance, naturally, therefore, looked upon the Baptists—dividing, as they supposed, the *one church* of Christ into many different sects—as its worst enemies, and the greatest barrier in the way of its realization. Hence they represented them as the sowers of the seeds of discord, strife, and confusion, the renders of the body of Christ, the foes of truth and order, peace and love; and, as such, they persecuted them with all the means which they could command.

To all the allegations against their polity, the Baptists might with propriety reply, that the fact that it was instituted by Christ, and recognized and adopted by the apostolic and primitive churches, is a sufficient proof of its excellence, and should be regarded by all as a satisfactory vindication. But they are not disposed thus summarily to deal with their opponents. They are willing, in the light of reason, guided by the word of God, calmly and dispassionately to consider their objections.

Baptists maintain that the church visible, as usually represented in the Holy Scriptures, is not a hierarchy, not an aggregation of all the professors of the true religion in the world, or in any kingdom, province, or city, but simply a local body of baptized believers, meeting statedly for the worship of God and the observance of the ordinances of his house. That, as a voluntary society, it is independent of all others, competent to transact its own business in its own way, according to the laws of Christ; under whom it is, in its own proper sphere, sovereign, binding and loosing with an authority from which there is no appeal to any tribunal but that of God. That, while owing obedience to "the powers that be," in matters purely civil and secular, and justly claiming their protection in the exercise of all its rights, it is essentially distinct and separate from the State, and, in its spiritual character and relations, wholly independent of it. That Christ is its only Head, its only and Supreme Ruler. That in religious rights and privileges its members are all equal. That among its ministers there is official parity. That although the apostles were superior in position to all other ministers of the first churches, their superiority did not descend to others. That, as a peculiar class of men, raised up for special purposes under extraordinary circumstances, which could only exist in their own times, they could have, in strictness, no successors. That in all matters of government and discipline, as well as of faith, the Word of God is the supreme law. That the administration of that law pertains to the church. That hence all claims of Papal supremacy, as well as all pretensions to prelatic, presbyterial, and synodical authority, are to be rejected.

In thus constituting and governing His church,

the Baptists see the most conspicuous exhibition of Divine wisdom and goodness. A vast overshadowing hierarchy, an all-embracing, all-absorbing, centralizing ecclesiasticism, they have ever regarded as fraught with evil. While it may have, what may seem to many, unity, strength, and grandeur, its unity will be apparent, rather than real, its strength carnal and human, rather than spiritual and divine, its grandeur subversive of the simplicity that is in Christ. The constant tendency of such a system is to corrupt the purity and destroy the integrity of the churches of Christ, to fetter and embarrass all the powers of the individual man, absorb his proper personality in the common mass, and even to destroy the liberties of the whole race. If one strong hand, like that of Hildebrand, should grasp the reins of power—if one strong will should get command of the mighty energies of the whole vast organism, what fearful rule might it not bear! Or, several ambitious and unscrupulous ecclesiastics conspiring and forming a spiritual oligarchy, how proudly and tyrannically might they not lord it over the heritage of God! Nor are these mere hypotheses. They have been realized, as the finest portions of the world, now and for ages withering under the influence of priestly domination, testify. How easily and rapidly, too, under such a system, might error, whether of faith or of practice, seizing upon some vital part, spread a destructive gangrene over every portion! Where there is no such vast and consolidated ecclesiasticism, no such centralizing hierarchy, however, the errors and abuses to which we have referred, if not impossible, are far less likely to arise. Each one of the many distinct and independent communities presents a breakwater, so to speak, against the tides of error and corruption, from any cause, or from any quarter, setting in, and checks, if it does not altogether arrest, their progress. Like the separate and sovereign States of the American Confederacy, balancing and regulating the Federal Government, and neutralizing any undue tendencies to consolidation, the separate and sovereign churches, counterbalancing centralizing tendencies (not less decided ecclesiastically than politically,) furnish the only proper pledges and sufficient guarantees of religious freedom.

Upon the Baptist theory, the church is to be viewed in a two-fold aspect, the one having respect to its divine, the other to its human relations. Regarded in the one aspect, it is a *theocracy;* regarded in the other, it is a pure *democracy.*

While, however, the church of Christ, considered in reference to its earthly relations alone, is a pure democracy, it is such a democracy as the world never before saw. It is not a democracy of the promiscuous, undisciplined, and lawless rabble. It is a democracy in which all the various classes of humanity are supposed to be represented in their highest types. A democracy of select men, each one of whom is presumed to understand the essential principles of truth and righteousness, and to be animated by a spirit of deep and inextinguishable devotion to them; and who, therefore, as a self-governed man, is prepared, with others like himself, to constitute a self-governed society.

If it be said that, however excellent the Baptist theory, it may never be realized; that in its practical development and application, grievous errors may be made; and that, in consequence, evils of the most serious character may result, we readily admit the force of the objection. But God must needs form a perfect theory—if he form a theory at all. And if, through human folly or human wickedness, it be not realized, surely it were very daring, by rejection of that theory, to seem to blame the infinitely wise and holy God. We protest against the charging upon a system divine and perfect in all its principles and in all its tendencies, the errors and imperfections of men. What is there in this world of error and of sin that men do not pervert and abuse?

We will still further admit that there are some evils incident to the administration of Baptist church polity, to which some other ecclesiastical organizations may not be so liable. Under this system, the individuality of man, his right of private judgment, the sanctity of his conscience, and his complete personal independence, are fully recognized. This may sometimes cause him to think more highly of himself than he ought to think, to turn his liberty into licentiousness, to strive to subject to his private judgment the general sense, and to exalt his individuality into supremacy over the whole church: thus may he cause strife, which may end in schism.

But other systems are just as liable to abuse—and to far greater abuse. Some of them greatly weaken, if they do not destroy all proper individuality of character, violate the sanctity of the individual conscience, disregard the right of private judgment, and subvert the proper personality and independence of the whole man. And these, we need not say, are evils of the greatest magnitude—evils from which the world has widely and woefully suffered, and from which the Baptist system, had it universally prevailed, would ever have saved it.

In that system, the democratic element is subordinated to the theocratic element. The church, as we have said, though *sovereign* with respect to its posture and bearings toward men, is *subject* with respect to its posture and bearings toward Christ. Its theocracy regulates and controls its democracy; so that with the bane, if there be such, in the workings of the Baptist system, goes along the antidote. Christ, the Head of his church, presiding over it, corrects its errors. The Head guides and controls the body.

The objection to what is supposed to be the *radical tendencies* of the Baptist church polity, has been often and strongly urged. This is an old charge revived. It was brought against the first Baptists. When they undermined the false foundations upon which men had built, their opponents contemptuously charged them with a seditious and revolutionary spirit, and said they "turned the world upside down."

The church polity of the Baptists is not more radical and revolutionary than the gospel itself. While fostering the aggressive and progressive spirit of that, it also fosters its spirit of moderation and conservatism. It goes no further than that. It goes no deeper than that. Its radicalism descends no lower than the foundations of truth. This is to be properly constructive, not destructive. It is to upbuild rather than to pull down. It is cementive rather than disruptive. Baptists think the want of a true radicalism one of the chief defects of their opponents. They do not go down to the granite foundations — they do not penetrate to and build upon the solid and eternal rock of divine truth, but base themselves superficially upon mere mounds of sand, upon heaps of the rubbish of antiquity, upon huge piles of human tradition—its wood, hay, and stubble, fit only to be burned. Well may many of them dread the Baptist radicalism. It will undermine and destroy their sandy foundations, as it did those of the ancient pharisaism of Judea and the ancient paganism of Rome.

Nor is the polity of the Baptists *agrarian* or *leveling* in its tendencies. The charge that it is so, originates, in many instances, far more in the defects of those who bring it, than in the polity to which they take exceptions, and might with equal force be urged against our elective franchise. Baptists make no war among the classes of society. They are themselves of all classes. While, as we should expect from the teachings of Christ and his Apostles, composed, for the most part, of the poor of this world, rich only in faith, they comprise many noble, and illustrious men, and "honorable women not a few." While now, as anciently, insisting upon humbleness of mind—a true and universal charity, they allow all to abide in the spheres in which they were originally called, whether they be high or low—the master or the servant, the peer or the peasant, the sovereign or the subject. And though, as members of the church, all are brethren, and one may not call another master; though all stand upon the same broad platform of equality in spiritual rights and privileges, there is no degradation of the strong to the level of the weak; of the educated, intelligent, and refined, to that of those circumstantially and essentially inferior. Some are always greater than the rest. Greater in faith, in prayer, and every good word and work —in force of moral and Christian character, and therefore greater in authority and influence among their brethren. "One star differ from another star in glory." Though the wisest and most efficient member of the fraternity may have a voice numerically only equal to that of him who is least so, the suffrage of the former may be really of an hundred times the weight of that of the latter.

Strifes and divisions occur more or less frequently in all communities of men, whether civil or religious, and because they are men, imperfect, erring, wicked men. In many instances, however, the very conflicts and divisions which occur among the Baptists, despite all the evils connected with them, furnish a noble illustration, and make the true eulogy of their polity. Though, on account of the popular nature of their system, the outspoken, independent character of their membership, and the absence of policy and cautious reserve, dissensions among them may become more readily and widely known than among some others, yet they are usually confined to the particular churches in which they arise, and do not involve the denomination at large.

A late writer strikingly remarks: "One of the beauties of the Baptist principle, taken as it undoubtedly is from the Bible, is that questions of strife can hardly by any possible means become *general*. The surges or ripples of discord, as the case may be, need something more human, as their conductors, than the universal spirit of love and union which connect all Christians together, and make them one in Christ Jesus. When these broad *systems* of human policy are wanting, as they are in our denominational belief, waves of strife must die abortive on their own narrow strand. They cannot ruffle or disturb the sea of Christian love."

A petty dispute, in a petty parish, has been known to embroil the whole English hierarchy. The misconduct of a single bishop has for years disturbed and embarrassed the Protestant Episcopal church of this country. A private feud between two prominent preachers, a few years since, convulsed with excitement one, if not two, of the largest and most influential Conferences of the Methodist Episcopal church South, and extended its baleful influences still more widely. "It was in great part by a single case of discipline, that the Presbyterian denomination in our country, was divided into the Old and New Schools. And this result," continues the writer, in whose words the statement is given, "grew out of the fact that a 'human' system of church government rendered it necessary, in the last resort, that the whole denomination should, by a judicatory higher than the local churches, review their proceedings, and confirm or reverse their action. Under such a polity, questions of strife must of necessity become general. But Baptists acknowledge no judicatory higher than the local churches. Here, if we be true to our principles, is a safeguard against *denominational* controversy on points which lie entirely within the jurisdiction of particular congregations. In these congregations, of right, the waves of strife rise and fall, sending not even the faintest ripple beyond." And when Baptists, true to their theory, "act in accordance with it, nothing can 'ruffle or disturb the sea of Christian love,' and drive the churches of the denomination apart, like a scattered fleet."

The existence of the *many sects* which assume, more or less modified, the Baptist name, because of an agreement with the Baptists in the one article of baptism, but which are really not identical with them, has often given occasion to their opponents, very unjustly, to charge the spirit of division and schism upon them. The existence of these numerous sects, agreeing with the Baptists in respect to the rite of baptism, but differing from them, in many other things, is rather an argument for the strength of their position, upon the question of baptism, than an argument for the weakness of their church polity. And this fact, thus furnishing a vindication of them from an unjust charge, and at the same time an independent and valuable argument in their favor, upon one of the chief points of controversy between them and others, we trust will be properly regarded, and constantly borne in mind by their opponents.

Some ecclesiastical communities have not life and energy enough for strife. They have neither interest in the great religious issues, nor independence and spirit enough for division. In others, a spiritual absolutism keeps down, or at least in the back-ground, the great body of the people, stifles the voice of the individual conscience, allows no liberty of speech or of action, and gives no room to an out-spoken and generous freedom of discussion. Hence their outward and apparent exemption from strifes and divisions. An exemption which, viewed in connection with its true cause, less honors than dishonors them, is far less their glory than their shame.

In respect to the charge of weakness and inefficiency in the Baptist polity, it may be said, that while the noble principle upon which every member of the church, without respect of persons, is individually recognized and honored, may be, as we have admitted, peculiarly liable to abuse by certain classes of character, that very principle proves the superior adaptation of this polity to the production and development of the greatest efficiency and strength.

The true theory of evangelization requires that each member of the church shall be a worker. He cannot be dispensed with. No one of the servants of Christ, however feeble or obscure, can be idle, without, to some extent, obstructing and retarding the progress of that great work which the Redeemer is carrying forward in the world. He fills a place that can be filled by no other. The Master has assigned to each his proper place, and said, "Occupy, till I come." And we believe that the conversion of the world to Christ will never be effected, until this theory of the gospel is practically carried out.

For rendering effective service, the private membership of the churches have, in some important respects, the advantage of the ministry. The former are, more completely than the latter, identified with all the various orders of society. Their position, habits, and pursuits, lead them to mingle more freely and unreservedly with them. Thus are they better prepared, in many instances, to act effectively upon them—to speak to them more in accordance with their peculiar modes of thought and feeling; to become truer exponents and interpreters of that thought and feeling. This is an advantage which can scarcely be too highly estimated. It gives to the churches a power analogous to that of those wondrous men of genius, who, "myriad-minded," embrace within themselves the types of all the orders of men, and who come as if special messengers from God, to speak to the people of all ages and of all lands; to remind them of their common nature, origin, and destiny; to counteract the tendencies to alienation of man from man, and class from class; and, by enkindling the same feelings, and awakening the same sentiments in all breasts, to unite mankind in the bonds of a common and universal brotherhood.

The efficiency of the early churches consisted not in their officers mainly, though some of them were Apostles, but in the whole body of the redeemed, each one of whom was a living stone in the spiritual temple, essential to its completeness, strength, and beauty; a living member of the spiritual body whose healthful and appropriate action was necessary to the full performance of all its functions.

Now, we maintain that by the polity of the Baptists, as by no other, is provision made for the practical realization of that true theory of evangelization, of which we have been speaking, and the accomplishment of the great work whose consummation it contemplates. Under it, each one's personal rights being respected, his sense of personal responsibility is aroused. All that is generous and noble in his character, is appealed to. He perceives that he is not lost in the common mass, that he is no mere puppet in the hands of others, to be used or not used as they please—that he may himself be something, and achieve something. Thus is he stimulated in the performance of his duty, and incited to a deep and self-denying devotion.

As to the objection that the separate and independent character of each church, is unfavorable to the exercise of the highest power of Christianity, it is, like others which we have noticed, by no means valid. That true unity which gives real strength, and produces the highest efficiency, comes from *within* rather than without. In the natural world, union between different bodies depends upon their having for each other inherent affinity, which no amount of outward force can create. Their union is chemical rather than mechanical. Without any external impulse, kindred substances, as if sentient and intelligent, seek each other out, and rush to each other's embrace; and so, in the spiritual world, things truly related, obeying superior impulses than those of gross and insensate matter, attract each other, and blend in the most beautiful accord. The true churches of Christ, however distinct and independent their several outward organizations, are essentially one. They breathe the same spirit, speak the same language, mind the same things. Their strong affinity for each other tends to an actual and outward development. Not more surely do the social and religious instincts of the individual Christian lead him to seek companionship with his Christian brother, than do similar instincts lead the individual church to seek communion and co-operation with its sister churches. Thus is secured, even outwardly, among the many distinct and independent communities of Baptists, that true unity for which Jesus prayed, and which he so tenderly and touchingly urged upon his people. These spiritual bodics—each in its proper sphere distinct, yet all under the gravitating force of mutual respect and love, identity of character, principles and aims, which binds each one to all the others, and the whole to the common centre, Christ—move in concentric circles, and thus exhibit something even more admirable than the wondrous unity and harmony displayed in the worlds and systems of worlds above us, in which simplicity and beauty, unity and strength, are so gloriously conjoined.

VII.

POSITION OF THE BAPTISTS.

Reflections against the Character and Position of the Baptists—Come with bad grace from their Opponents—Number and Diffusion of the Baptists—Cultivation and Intelligence among them—Allegation that their Churches are composed of the Poor of the World unworthy serious Reply—Their social and general Position.

IT is sometimes disdainfully said that the Baptists are poor, illiterate, few in number, devoid of social refinement, and occupy an unimportant position in the world. The reflections thus cast upon them, however potent their influence upon many minds, we regard as in themselves altogether trivial. We might, perhaps, find a fitting and sufficient reply to those who cast these unworthy reflections, in the words of Nazianzen to those by whom he and his brethren were contemned: "Where are those who reproach us with our poverty, who define the church by the multitude, and despise the little flock? They have the people, but we the faith."[1]

[1] In Orat. Arian. et pro seipso—as cited by Chillingworth.

Neither wealth, nor learning, nor numbers, nor social position, nor courtliness of manners, nor worldly influence, have any necessary connection with piety, or the favor of God. If they have, then the Apostles, and other early Christians, possessed neither. They were fewer in numbers, poorer, more illiterate, more deeply depressed socially, than the Baptists now are, even in the view of our most prejudiced opponents.

While coming with very bad grace from those whose ecclesiastical ancestry did so much to depress and destroy the Baptists, such uncharitable statements, as we have mentioned, are not only in themselves trivial, but groundless. The Baptists of the present day are much more highly favored than their despised and persecuted predecessors. The lines are fallen to them in pleasant places. They have a goodly heritage. The little one has become a thousand, the small one a strong nation. The Lord has hastened it in his time.

Wherever Baptists have been allowed scope for development they show what, under auspicious circumstances, they would have been, and would have done, in all ages, and in all lands. Since they have obtained freedom to worship God according to the dictates of their own consciences, and to "sit every man under his vine and under his fig tree, none making him afraid," they have wonderfully advanced in numbers, in wealth, in cultivation, in social position, in general influence upon the world.

In regard to numbers, it cannot now be said as it has so often been sneeringly done, that the Baptists are "a mere handful." In the United States, where they now have what they never before had in any age or country, a wide and unobstructed field, they are developing the inherent power of their principles, and displaying something of that elastic and expansive energy, which the heavy hand of oppression and persecution so long suppressed, but could not destroy.

From about the middle of the last century, to the American Revolution, though they then labored under many and great disadvantages, being persecuted both in the North and in the South, by the ruling ecclesiastical parties, they increased in this country from about *one in every four hundred* of the population, to about *one in every sixty*. Since the Revolution, they have increased from *one in sixty*, to *one in twenty*—now numbering, including all who hold their fundamental principles, *a million and a half of actual communicants*, about *seven and a half millions of adherents*,—(one-fourth of the population of our great Confederacy,)—and having about *a quarter of all the church accommodation in the whole country*. While equal, numerically, to the Methodists, strictly counted,—they are more than twice the number of the Presbyterians, and more than ten times that of the Episcopalians.

In England and Wales, they are one of the most important bodies of Dissenters from the Established Church. In France, though almost exterminated, along with the other opponents of the Papacy, by the Revocation of the Edict of Nantes, they still exist. And though their churches are few and feeble, and subjected by their enemies to constant embarrassments, their sentiments are widely, though as yet not very openly, spreading. Suppressed in Germany, by persecution suffered at the hands of the Lutherans as well as of the Romanists, they have at length re-appeared. And notwithstanding great opposition and sore persecution, they have increased, in about a score of years, from *seven* to more than *seven thousand*. They exist, in considerable numbers, in Holland, where, within the present century, the king offered them the patronage of the State, though, true to their principles, they declined the proffered grace. They are found in Denmark and in Norway, in Sweden and in Switzerland. In Sweden, though embarrassed greatly by the opposition of the ministers of the State Church, and by many civil disabilities, they are rapidly rising into importance.

In India, the Baptists have many churches and communicants. They have established themselves in China and Central Africa, have commenced a mission to Japan, and another to Brazil. In Liberia they have several mission stations and flourishing churches. In the West Indies are some of their strongest churches. In the flourishing English colony of Australia, their principles are now having a wide diffusion. Among the American Indians they have done a noble work in the translation of the Scriptures, the formation of churches, and the establishment of schools.

Thus scattered throughout the world, set up as lights in the midst of the darkness of every great section of the earth, they are witnessing now, as of old, under good report and evil report, amid obloquy and scorn, opposition and persecution.

Nor are they, as compared with other Christian communities, justly chargeable with want of cultivation and intelligence. Referring to the Baptists of the time of Cromwell and the Commonwealth, William R. Williams says, " In literature, it is honor enough that our sentiments were held by the two men who displayed, beyond all comparison, the most creative genius, in that age of English literature, Milton and Bunyan."[1] One of the most accomplished oriental scholars, as well as one of the ablest expositors of the Holy Scriptures, during the last century, was John Gill. The scholar who was deemed, in his day, the profoundest ori-

[1] Miscellanies, Life and Times of Baxter, p. 202.

entalist alive, was Yates of Calcutta. The man who, as a translator of the Scriptures, has been called the Tyndale of modern times, who during the forty years of his labors in India, in connection with his associates, published two hundred and twelve thousand volumes of the Bible, in forty different languages, and of whom the venerable John Newton said, "I look to such a man with reverence—he is more to me than bishop or archbishop, he is an apostle,"[1] was William Carey. And the man who, as a translator, deserves, in some respects, a higher place than Carey—a man whose version of the Bible in Burmese, is pronounced by Burman scholars, "*perfect as a literary work*,"[2] was Adoniram Judson. The profoundest, most judicious, and most reliable theologian of the generation just gone by, a writer whom Dr. Campbell of London styles the "Bacon of Scripture," who "traverses with giant steps the whole empire of Revelation and of reason as its hand-maid," and of whose works he says that they are "in themselves a Library," and, "with the Bible, will suffice to make any man a first rate theologian," was Andrew Fuller. The most original and able essayist of the present generation, was John Foster. Its most finished pulpit orator, and, at the same time, a writer who united to the elegance, and much more than the strength and splen-

[1] Anderson's History of the English Bible, p. 504.
[2] Wayland's Life of Judson, vol. ii. p. 167.

dor of Addison, the purity of Swift, and the loftiness of Johnson, was Robert Hall. One of the most accomplished philologists of our times, a writer who has forever settled, in its philological relations at least, that long and hotly contested question, of the meaning of the word Βαπτιζω, a thinker who has won the title of the Jonathan Edwards of the nineteenth century, was the late Alexander Carson. The author of the ablest exposition of that most difficult portion of the New Testament, the Epistle to the Romans, was Robert Haldane.

If it comported with our sense of delicacy and propriety to speak of the living as we have done of the dead, we might easily show that among eminent living scholars and philosophers, writers and preachers, Baptists hold no mean rank. We might point to a preacher who rivals Whitefield—to an ethical philosopher superior to Paley—to a writer who combines the grace and delicate beauty of Washington Irving with much of the felicity and wealth of illustration of Macaulay—to scholars of a richer and profounder lore than that of Porson or of Bentley.

There are other and yet more satisfactory evidences of the injustice of the charge now under review. They are furnished by the universities, colleges, theological seminaries, and other schools innumerable, of the Baptists, for the culture and training both of males and females. They are furnished by the thousands of books and other publications of high character, constantly issuing from their presses. They are furnished in the pulpit, in the pew, in the social circle, in every sphere of business, in every walk of life.

The allegation that their churches are composed of the poor of the world, we consider unworthy serious notice. God has so blessed them, temporally, as well as spiritually, that we could easily demonstrate that the aggregate of wealth among them is far greater than that of some ecclesiastical fraternities, whose members not unfrequently put on lordly airs, and affect to despise the Baptists for their poverty. But to a task like this we are unwilling to descend.

With respect to the charge that the social position of the Baptists is humble, it might be well to inquire by what standard do those who bring it judge. We think that "Christian is the highest style of man." That the truer the Christian, the truer the gentleman. That the nearer one approaches Christ, the higher on the true scale he rises; and that the further he recedes from him, the lower he sinks. Tried by this standard, the Baptists, we trust, would bear comparison with others.

Nor, to view the matter in *the light of their opponents,* are the Baptists so depressed as is charged. As we have said, they are of all classes.

We have seen that genius the most illustrious, learning the most profound, piety the most exalted, are theirs. That though charged with poverty, they are by no means devoid of wealth. That amiability and refinement—in a word, that all the elements of the highest social character and standing may be found among them.

If, then, the Baptists be so widely diffused as we have stated; if they possess the numbers, the intelligence, the zeal, the energy, the wealth, the piety which we have ascribed to them, it were impossible that their position in the world should be so unimportant as their opponents allege. Nor is it. In many respects, the position of no people is more important; and, as we shall see in the following section, the influence of none greater.

VIII.

INFLUENCE OF THE BAPTISTS.

Want of Correspondence between their Claims and their Achievements urged against the Baptists—Mission of the Baptists—Its Extent and Difficulty—Mightiest enterprises often carried forward upon scale of imperceptible gradations—Baptists have achieved more than superficially appears—Have "wrought rather than written"—What they have done—Primitive Baptists—Medieval Baptists—Modern Baptists.

IF the claims of the Baptists be just, why is it that they have had no greater success in the world? why have they not figured more in the history of the past? why are they not now more numerous, more prominent, more influential? These are questions often tauntingly put by the opponents of the Baptists, and are well worthy the consideration of their friends.

To the casual and superficial observer, the Baptists may seem to have essentially failed in the great mission upon which they profess to have been sent. But that they have not, will appear, if we take a just and sufficiently comprehensive view.

The mission of the Baptists is of the grandest and most difficult character. It is nothing less than the conquest of a world. It is the conversion to their principles of the whole human race. We cannot accept the views of those, who, regarding the true mission of the Baptists as a work of almost exclusive bearing upon *certain classes of men*, would seem to us greatly too much to limit and lower that mission. No! we believe the mission of the Baptists is coextensive and identical with that of the gospel itself. Theirs is the broad commission—"Go, teach all nations, baptizing them in the name of the Father, and of the Son, and of the Holy Ghost." And in its fulfillment theirs is the promise—"Lo, I am with you alway, even unto the end of the world." The true mission of the Baptists, then, is wide as the world, durable as time—a mission to all them that dwell on the earth, to every kindred and tribe and people under the whole heaven. To men of the most diverse character, culture, and circumstances—from the prince to the peasant, from the most fastidious and courtly gentlemen of the city, to the rudest boor of the wilds.

We have no notion that others can, as some suppose, preach the gospel more effectively to the proud, the worldly, the rich, the refined, the intellectual. Those who have most of the truth, and the spirit of the truth, are most competent ably and successfully to preach it. But, with all the difficulties that lie in the way, to convert all orders of men from their multiform errors and sins, to a system of perfect truth and immaculate purity, is to effect infinitely the greatest and most arduous work-ever attempted on the earth; and it cannot be done in a day.

It is not accordant with the ordinary principles of the divine economy to work otherwise than by what might seem to men somewhat slow processes, and upon a scale, in many instances, of almost imperceptible gradations. Thus he created the world, gradually evolving from the wildest and crudest materials, a system of marvelous harmony of parts and order of operations. Only after long months of preparation, does the God of nature bring out from the bare bleak winter, the bud of spring, the bloom of summer, and the golden grain of autumn. He whose life is eternity can afford to take time. "He does not drive all his work into any one year. Amid delays and struggles, he holds through every hour, dark or light, of every day, in every year, His sleepless post of observant guardianship, and retains His unrelaxing grasp of the helm of universal dominion."

"Never does he haste—
Never does he rest."

We believe that Christianity has often moved

forward when it seemed to stand still. Nay, that while seeming to retrograde, it has made a true progress—a progress which all, if they saw as God sees, would readily recognize. It has stooped to bound higher. It has stepped back to "gain a purchase" for a more successful effort, a surer and more rapid advance. "Now and then there has been a stoppage, now and then a short retrogression, but as to the general tendency there can be no doubt. A single breaker may recede, but the tide is evidently coming in." The natural Israel were a type of the spiritual Israel. The long residence and deep depression of the former, in the land of Ham, their marching and counter-marching in the wilderness, before their entrance into the land of promise, were typical and illustrative of the career and fortunes of the latter.

The partial and temporary failure of his people, is doubtless designed and ordained by God, to prepare them for ultimate and complete success. Their reverses are necessary, it may be, to give them a proper view of the difficulties and dangers of their position, the number and strength of their adversaries—above all, to impress them with a due sense of their dependence upon the Divine Power, and to enable them to realize the truth of that blessed paradox—"When I am weak, then am I strong."

He to whom a thousand years are but as a day,

a world but as an atom, lays his plans for the infinite. He allows wicked men and institutions long to continue, that, in the view of all his intelligent creation, they may thoroughly evolve all the evil within them, solve the problems of sin and error, for the instruction and profit of the *whole universe*, for *all eternity*. Thus the mouths of gainsayers shall be finally and forever shut, and all the workers of iniquity put to perpetual shame. Thus the righteous, however for a time disheartened, shall at last have their cause firmly and eternally established. If evil principles were at once suppressed, limited in their range, or fettered in their operation, they might be thought less injurious than *an expenditure of their whole energy, under circumstances the most favorable to their development*, would prove them to be. Nay, the enemies of God might even affirm that they were not injurious at all, but only seemed so because of their circumscribed and embarrassed action—that had they been allowed to operate longer, and on a field wider and worthier, they would have shown themselves good and not evil. Men wonder that He who is " a jealous God," and who will not give his glory to another, should allow idolatry to continue for a day. But idolatry must solve its problem. It must teach the universe its lesson—its lesson for eternity. Idolatry, then, must have time to give its lesson. It must show itself under all its possible forms and phases. It must go as high as it can, and as far—and it must sink to the lowest deep to which it can go down. So of all the forms of error and of sin which have existed in the world.

On the other hand, truth must be put to the test. Virtue must be tried. They too must give their lesson to the universe—their lesson for eternity. And to do it, they also must have time.

Taking the whole career of the Baptists into view, it might appear that they have achieved, or gotten into a position to achieve, far more than would appear in a more limited range of vision. "The men who originate the most important movements, seldom are the men to record them. Those who achieve the materials for history, seldom stop to write them down. Thus far Baptists have wrought rather than written. They have dug a deep foundation, running under ground through the history of Christianity in the world, and resting on the Rock of Ages. But as a denomination they have not occupied its pages with a description of the lofty erections which they have reared. As in the construction of some large building it takes months to dig away the rubbish, and lay the foundations firm, so that the building seems long in reaching the level of the surrounding earth, while after that, it soon appears as a lofty edifice that shall stand for ages; so thus far the progress of the Baptists has been slow and laborious, while removing errors and prejudices from the minds of nations, so as to get a clear space and settled foundation, upon which to build. But that work accomplished, the rest becomes certain, easy, and enduring. As the historian, Neander, once remarked, 'There is a future for the Baptists.'"[1]

That they have already effected a great work, have fulfilled an important part of their high mission, we cannot doubt. What have they done? Taking the view which we have all along taken, that they are the true representatives and successors of the first followers of Christ, then, whatever may have been their subsequent delinquencies, much of the honor is theirs, under God, of the marvelous achievements of the apostolic and primitive churches, in disseminating evangelic truth, and establishing the cause of Christ throughout the whole known world, in the face of the combined opposition of Jew and Gentile, Greek and Barbarian, earth and hell,—and this, though they were few in number, without worldly influence, and, for the most part, poor, illiterate, and despised.

And if, in this view, it be said that the guilt and shame of the great apostasy, with its egregious errors and its awful crimes, attaches to the Baptists—that the church of Rome was a Baptist

[1] Curtis' Prog. Bap. Principles, pp. 367, 368

church, and its bishop a Baptist pastor—that the servile and obsequious churches and pastors of the provinces, which acknowledged the supremacy of, and crouched before, the proud and imperious church of the metropolis, were Baptist churches—that they suffered to come, if they did not bring, upon the world, the thousand years of night, with all its horrors—that its rank growth of deadly nightshade, its flocks of obscene and ill-omened birds, its nests of envenomed reptiles, its dreariness and gloom, its chill and stupor, its noxious, death-diffusing exhalations, must be regarded in some sense Baptist products,—we reply, that, these objections against the Baptists would be equally objections against Christianity itself,—and that, even if they were just, many circumstances of extenuation might be pleaded. The first followers of Christ were a noble band, of whom the world was not worthy. They were distinguished by every public and private virtue. How unselfish, how self-denying, were they! How deeply devoted to God! How loving towards each other! How magnanimous towards their enemies! How compassionate and kind to the weak, the helpless, the suffering! How fearless in circumstances of extremest and most appalling peril! How they glowed with pure and unquenchable zeal! What sublime energy did they display! What perseverance! What fortitude! The whole world was arrayed against them. No weapon save the sword of the Spirit, which is the word of God, was in their hands. That blade of celestial temper, however, was resistless. It blazed with a strange unearthly light—a light that irradiated the darkest hovels of the poor, that penetrated into the deepest dens of iniquity, that burst into the marble halls of the Cæsars, that revealed the abominations of the pagan priest, in the inner shrine of the pagan temple, paled the unhallowed fires on its altars, and dispelled the black clouds of its incense forever. Wherever gleamed the Roman sword, there gleamed this two-edged sword of the Spirit. Wherever perched the Roman eagle, wherever its proud eyrie was built, there brooded the Holy Dove, there was consecrated its holy place. Rome herself, imperial, arrogant, and unused to submission, at length confessed and yielded to the power of warriors mightier and more invincible than her own. The statues of her gods were broken. Her Pantheon was demolished. The Christian temple towered upon the ruins of that of Jupiter Stator. The cross, once the symbol of shame, became the badge of honor, worn near the heart of woman, on the breast of the chivalrous knight, and emblazoned on the flaunting banner of the victorious army.

But, in this very success the early Christians found disaster and defeat. By their heroism and their hardihood, by their unparalleled virtues of every kind, by their marvelous successes, they achieved temporal as well as spiritual glory. They won an earthly name. They secured power and place among men. And, to say nothing of the terrible trial to their own integrity, which all this honor caused—a trial perhaps the hardest of all trials for humanity to bear—it opened upon them the floodgates of all corruption from without. Hordes of hypocrites pressed into the churches. The time-serving, the self-seeking, those whose fortunes had been wrecked, and whose hopes had been blighted, by folly or by crime, bold and unprincipled adventurers—all, in a word, who were willing to make a gain of godliness, and all who, like drift-wood, follow the course of every high and sweeping current, sought the society and alliance of the people of God. They, warmed and elated by success, glowing with enthusiasm, and, from their own very simplicity, conscious honesty, and rectitude of purpose, disinclined to look suspiciously upon any—and, in many instances, doubtless, too eager to make proselytes—with open arms welcomed, without proper scrutiny and wise precaution, these professed converts. Throwing wide the doors of the church, they admitted into the fold of Christ these wolves in sheep's clothing. Satan himself, changing his tactics, became a preacher of righteousness. He ceased to be the accuser of the brethren, and became their advocate. He transformed himself into an angel of light. Nay, in the person of his human representative, he, as God, sat in the temple of God, showing himself that he was God. Thus, all unperceived, and almost before its best and wisest friends had more than suspicion of it, radical and essential change had taken place. The church of God had given place to the synagogue of Satan. Truth fell prostrate in the streets. Every movement for reform was suppressed. Every voice that was raised in remonstrance was silenced.

In truth, then, if this view be just, the great apostasy, so called, was, in strictness, no apostasy at all. It was not the defection of the true people of God. They doubtless made mistakes. They doubtless sinned. And deeply did they suffer for it. But they were still, and to the last, loyal to their King. That so-called apostasy was but the natural and necessary development of the essential principle and spirit of those who, while among God's people, were not really of them—those who had "stolen the livery of the court of Heaven to serve the devil in." It was but the apparent and temporary triumph of the powers of darkness, permitted by God, in part, it may be, to rebuke the mistakes of policy, and punish other and worse delinquencies of his people; in part, to teach them their own weakness, the subtilty, and strategy, and strength of the great Adversary, and their constant and absolute dependence upon a higher and mightier than human aid.

But, as we have already seen in a previous portion of this work, God did not leave himself, in those dark days, without a witness on the earth. Amid innumerable false, many were still true. In some instances, perhaps, they had an outward and nominal connection with the enemies of God. But it was a connection involuntary and constrained. There was no spiritual and real affiliation. The oil and the water flowed along in the same channel; but they were oil and water still. Hence, from time to time, as opportunity offered, in opposition to the enemy that had come in as a flood, a standard was set up and bravely sustained, till overwhelming odds coming against it, death paralyzed the hand by which it was upheld. Of such revolts against the established hierarchy there are many records. And, without question, there would have been many more, had not that hierarchy, as we have said, held the pen as well as the sword.

Even in the very midnight of the ages, when the powers of darkness seemed supreme, there were many more than seven thousand men who had not bowed the knee to the Baal of Rome, and whom God concealed, and would not suffer to be touched. These, for the most part, we have shown were essentially Baptist in principle and in spirit.

Now these poor people, despised and afflicted,

whose names were cast out as evil, and who, whenever and wherever they appeared, were driven out from before the face of men, into the wilderness, the clefts of the rocks, the dens and caves of the earth—these men were the salt of the earth, at the time of its deepest corruption—the light of the world, when the world most needed light.

Who, then, shall say that, even when weakest and most depressed, the Baptists failed? Failed! Nay, they were then doing, in some respects, their greatest work. Alone, they were keeping the bridge of truth, against the overwhelming odds of error. They were standing in the Thermopylæ of the ages. They were throwing themselves into the terrible breach that had been made, by the hosts of hell, in the walls of Zion. And they saved Zion.

We do not know but that dark as is this portion of the Christian ages, it is, in some aspects of it, the most interesting of them all. Perhaps, too, it was as important as any of them to the final success and permanent establishment of Christianity. In the economy of nature, winter is as important as spring, night as necessary as day, clouds as indispensable as sunshine. In winter, nature is not dead, nor asleep, nor inactive. In the inner chambers of her great laboratory, she is busily and effectively at work. She is preparing for all those wonderful transformations which the advancing year shall disclose, when the flower shall bud and bloom in mead and valley, the grass grow green over hill and dale, the forests come forth in gorgeous sheen, and all imprisoned life find full enlargement. So, in the economy of grace, wintry seasons, seasons of darkness, are not necessarily fruitless. They may be seasons of a true inward and spiritual activity, seasons of real progress, however inappreciable by the common eye.

During those gloomy ages, our Baptist forefathers were preparing the way of the Reformers. They were erecting the pedestals on which stand the colossal figures of Luther and Melancthon, Calvin and Zuinglius, with their illustrious compeers,—pedestals, however, far grander and more enduring than the statues surmounting them. It was they who had, under God, made the Reformation possible. "Their views," says Underhill, "formed the ultimate idea of the great movement of the Reformation."[1] Arnold of Brescia, an earnest opponent of infant baptism, and a noble champion of liberty, sacred and secular, "produced an immense effect upon Europe and his age, and gave an impulse to those reforming movements in the church of Rome, that are distinctly traceable as the germs from which, four hundred years later, sprang the great Protestant Reformation."[2] Others, like him, hold-

[1] Rel. Lib. p. 194.
[2] Curtis' Prog. Bap. Prin., p. 24.

ing the great primordial principle of the Baptists, that "the church can consist only of holy and pious persons," contributed equally to that grand result. "In times of ignorance and unbelief," says the German theologian Knapp, "they have been the depositaries of uncorrupted Christianity. Without the Waldenses, the Wickliffites, and the Hussites, the Reformation would not have taken place."[1] Gibbon says, "The visible assemblies of the Paulicians, or Albigeois, were extirpated by fire and sword; and the bleeding remnant escaped by flight, concealment, or Catholic conformity. But the invincible spirit which they had kindled, still lived and breathed in the western world. In the state, in the church, and even in the cloister, a latent succession was preserved of the disciples of St. Paul, who protested against the tyranny of Rome, embraced the Bible as the rule of faith, and purified their creed from all the visions of the Gnostic theology. The struggles of Wickliffe in England, of Huss in Bohemia, were premature and ineffectual; but the names of Zuinglius, Luther, and Calvin are pronounced with gratitude as the deliverers of nations."[2] The authors of the History of the Reformed Church of the Netherlands say, "Before the name of Luther as a Reformer

[1] Christian Theology, p. 474.

[2] Milman's Gibbon, vol. v. pp. 398, 399.

was known, it appears that the Anabaptists in this land carried on the work of Reformation, originally undertaken by others, and drew many from the Romish church to them, and rebaptized them. Had these Anabaptists then possessed really learned men, how great would have been the harvest reaped from the good seed which they had scattered! In all probability all the light which now shines in Europe would have emanated from their community, and at a much earlier period."[1]

The constant persecutions to which they were exposed, and the denial to them, so far as was possible, of all the means of mental culture and development, were the cause of their want of "really learned men." But, despite all difficulties, they had still kept burning, however remotely and obscurely, the fires of truth and freedom, at which was lighted the torch of many a brave Reformer, who bore it blazing in the darkness far and wide. The great principles of the supreme authority of the Holy Scriptures, justification by faith, the right of private judgment, and all the doctrines that made the Reformation popular and successful, they had always held.

Thus, long before the time of Luther, had the

[1] Hist. Neth. Ref. Ch., Translation in S. Bap. Rev., April, 1859.

Baptists sowed the seed of the great harvest of Reform. And although, when just springing up and adorning with living green the fields of Central and Western Europe, it sometimes seemed about to be destroyed, it did not die. God himself threw over it his mantle, which, while concealing, protected it. The snows of winter lay thick upon it, not to blight, but to preserve, till, in due time, under the genial influence of softer skies and brighter suns, balmier airs and more refreshing showers, the fields white unto the harvest, the grain ripe for the sickle, the great Reapers should come. Then stepped forth Luther and his compeers; and at once, to speak without a figure, they found a people prepared. Hence it was that so soon after they raised the standard of reform, so many millions rallied around it.

If these views be just, then, to the Baptists rightly belongs no little of the credit of the Reformation, and of the glorious results to truth and freedom, civil and religious, which have flowed from that mighty movement of the human mind.

But greater credit still is theirs. For had the Reformers been as consistent and thorough-going as they, the work of Reformation had not stopped where it did, in mid-career. It had not so soon declined. It had not so soon itself needed reformation. There would not be room, at this late day, for saying in reference to it, as a distinguished follower of Luther, the Chevalier Bunsen, has said, "The question at this moment is, not *how to carry out*, but *how to prepare, a second, grand, reconstructive Reformation.* The porch of the temple must first be more thoroughly cleansed than it was in the sixteenth, and, above all, restored more honestly than it was in the seventeenth, century; and, lastly, the work must be handled more practically than has yet been done by the critical German school of this age."[1] Nor would the followers of Luther now maintain that "the body and blood of Christ are actually present in the bread and wine of the sacrament." They would not retain "the rites of confession, absolution, and exorcism," and allow "the use of images in worship." They would not be, as they are, but "little less intolerant toward other forms of Protestantism than Romanism itself." They would not be, as "in Sweden, the support of an absolute despotism." Their clergy would not "have the control of the people, in all the circumstances and relations of life, and leave them scarcely a vestige of personal freedom."

Since the era of the Reformation, when the Baptists first came forth from their long and deep retreats—the woman emerging from the wilderness

[1] Hippolytus and his Age, vol. ii. Int. p. 18: 2d ed., London, 1854.

—though they have constantly labored under many disadvantages, they have made great progress, and exerted broadly upon the world an influence of the highest and most beneficial character.

In the Netherlands, they aided the great Prince of Orange in his struggle with the bloody bigot of Spain, and thus contributed effectively to the establishment of the Dutch Republic, and to the mighty influence which it exerted in behalf of human freedom throughout the world. When William's affairs wore their gloomiest aspect, when his most powerful friends failed him, when his coffers were empty, and his cause seemed desperate, they came, bringing their hard-earned savings and their earnest sympathies, to his relief. Of this statement, there are most affecting illustrations. "A poor Anabaptist preacher collected a small sum from a refugee congregation on the outskirts of Holland, and brought it, at the peril of his life, into the Prince's camp. It came from people, he said, whose will was better than the gift. They never wished to be repaid, he said, except by kindness, when the cause of reform should be triumphant in the Netherlands. The Prince signed a receipt for the money, expressing himself touched by this sympathy from these poor outcasts. In the course of time, other contributions from similar sources, principally collected by dissenting preachers, starving and persecuted church communities, were received. The poverty-stricken exiles contributed far more, in proportion, for the establishment of civil and religious liberty, than the wealthy merchants or haughty nobles."[1]

In England, the Baptists have long made themselves known and felt in every department of the realm. They assisted Cromwell and the Parliament in crushing the tyranny of the Stuarts. Baxter, an ardent royalist as well as Pedobaptist, and objecting as much to the political as to the religious opinions of the Baptists, ascribed to them "the chief events which hurried on the subversion of monarchy and the establishment of a republic." They filled Cromwell's armies with "preaching, and praying, and valiant men." And when Cromwell gave signs of himself playing the tyrant, they boldly withstood him. In their preaching, in their writings, in their lives, free or in chains, in the dungeon or on the scaffold, they heroically maintained their principles. "In the cause of religious and political freedom, it was the lot of our community to labor, none the less effectively because they did it obscurely, with Keach, doomed to the pillory, or, like Delaune, perishing in the dungeon. The opinions, as to religious freedom, then professed by our churches, were not only denounced by statesmen as rebellion, but by grave divines as

[1] Motley's Rise of the Dutch Republic, vol. ii. pp. 250, 251.

the most fearful heresy. Through evil and through good report they persevered, until what had clothed them with obloquy, became, in the hands of later scholars and more practiced writers, as Locke, a badge of honór and a diadem of glory. Nor should it be forgotten, that these views were not with them, as with some others, professed in the time of persecution and virtually retracted when power had been won. Such was, alas, the course of names no less illustrious than Stillingfleet and Taylor. But the day of prosperity and political influence was with our churches the day for their most earnest dissemination. Their share in shoring up the falling liberties of England, and in infusing new vigor and liberality into the constitution of that country, is not yet generally acknowledged. It is scarce even known. The dominant party in the church and the state, at the Restoration, became the historians; and 'when the man, and not the lion, was thus the painter,' it was easy to foretell with what party all the virtues, all the talents, and all the triumphs would be found. When our principles shall have won their way to more general acceptance, the share of the Baptists in the achievements of that day will be disinterred, like many other forgotten truths, from the ruins of history. Then it will, we believe, be found, that while dross, such as has alloyed the purest churches in the best ages, may have been found in some of our denomination, yet the body was composed of pure and scriptural Christians, who contended manfully, some with bitter sufferings, for the rights of conscience and the truth as it is in Jesus; that to them English liberty owes a debt it has never acknowledged; and that amongst them Christian freedom found its earliest and some of its staunchest, its most consistent, and its most disinterested champions."[1]

But it is in the United States that the Baptists, since the Reformation, have made the greatest progress, and exercised the widest and strongest influence. Here they have a congenial clime, a large and open field, rich soil, and every facility for its cultivation.

In the establishment of the free institutions which are the glory of the American people, they performed a most important part. In Virginia, the most populous and influential of the colonies, they enthusiastically rallied around the great orator, whose voice crying, "Give me liberty or give me death!" was arousing the people to resistance of British oppression.

And as in Virginia, so throughout the whole country, they everywhere espoused the cause of freedom. When the war commenced, their sons enlisted in the army, and their ministers acted as

[1] W. R. Williams' Miscellanies, pp. 202, 203.

its chaplains. "The Baptists," says Backus, "were so generally united with their country in the defense of its privileges, that when the General Court at Boston, passed an act in October, 1778, to debar all men from returning into their government whom they judged to be their enemies, and named three hundred and eleven men as such, there was not one Baptist among them. Yet there was scarce a Baptist member in the Legislature which passed this act."[1]

But not only was their influence felt on the field. It was equally felt in the council. The first Continental Congress, held in Philadelphia, 1774, had not been in session ten days before they presented a memorial setting forth that they "united with their country in defense of its privileges," and beseeching its assembled representatives to secure at once the recognition of the inalienable rights of conscience. In behalf of these rights, they presented other memorials and addresses, some of which are eminently distinguished for clearness of statement, force of argument, and eloquence of expression.

"They were to a man," says an able writer in the Baptist Family Magazine, "the friends of liberty, both civil and religious, and the friends of liberty gradually recognized and honored

[1] Hist. N. E. Baptists, in Bap. Lib., vol. i. p. 160.

them. In Virginia, they overthrew the persecuting hierarchy, by patient suffering and persevering testimony to the truth. Patrick Henry, Jefferson, Madison, and Washington aided their efforts. The constitution of Virginia was moulded on their principles of religious liberty in 1776. The North Western Territory, ceded by Virginia to the Union, by the ordinance of 1787, was set apart to the same principles forever. The Constitution of the United States was amended in 1789, so as to prohibit Congress ever to legalize a religious establishment, or to invade the rights of conscience in any manner or degree. This was a grand triumph of Baptist principles in this country; or more properly of New Testament principles, for which alone Baptists have pleaded and suffered. It was a national acknowledgment of the authority of Jesus Christ over his own kingdom in the human soul. Such an acknowledgment, no nation, as such, had ever made before. It was a new era in the world's history. It was the beginning of a new epoch in Christendom."

The influence of the Baptists, so great upon the civil institutions of our country, has been, notwithstanding the determined resistance encountered, yet greater upon its religious establishments. It has changed the whole character and aspect of American Christianity. "The practices of our brethren around us have burst the restraints of their written formularies, and some of them have but to state their positions to their own consciousness, and they are Baptists at once."[1] Indeed, Bushnell, Mines, Nevin, and others confess that several of the leading Pedobaptist denominations of the country are, to say the least, "*Semi-Baptist.*" This acknowledgment on the part of prominent Pedobaptists, whether intended as such or not, may be justly claimed as a tribute to the influence of the Baptists.

That all these denominations powerfully feel the pressure of that influence, is evident from many considerations. We name only one. It is that of the ever-weakening hold, upon the minds and hearts of their membership, of that doctrine which has been always the main support of their ecclesiastical systems. While in all European countries where there are no Baptists, or where from any cause their influence is slight, all, or nearly all the children are baptized, in the United States, where the Baptists are so numerous and their influence so great, "*not one child in ten receives the rite.*" Throughout the whole country, and we think mainly through the influence of the Baptists, under God, infant baptism, that bane of Christianity, is "waxing old, effete, and ready to vanish away."

We state these things in no boastful or unchari-

[1] Cutting's Hist. Vind., p. 52.

table spirit, but as simple matters of fact, strikingly illustrative of the extent and power of that influence of the Baptists which so many affect to despise, and of which they so slightingly speak.

But, though the influence of the Baptists, in modern times, has been and still is greatest in England and the United States, the two freest and most enlightened nations of the world, it is by no means confined to them. At this moment it is powerfully felt in every quarter of the world. They have been the leaders in the great enterprise of modern missions to the heathen. "In the year 1784, at a Baptist Association held at Nottingham, it was determined that one hour on the first Monday evening of every month should be devoted to solemn and special intercession for the revival of genuine religion, and for the extension of the kingdom of Christ throughout the world; hence the origin of Monthly Missionary Prayer Meetings,"[1] whose vast and blessed influence, for the last three quarters of a century, in keeping alive the missionary spirit at home, and carrying forward the missionary work abroad, no finite mind can estimate.

In his work on India as a Field of Missions, Macleod Wylie, speaking of the Baptists, says—"Without any reference to their operations or influence elsewhere, it is but fair to say that to them,

[1] Harris' Great Commission, p. 161.

above all other Christian bodies, this part of India (Bengal) is deeply indebted. Not only have their churches in Great Britain and America sent out some of the most distinguished missionaries who ever preached the gospel—for such certainly were Carey, Marshman, and Ward, Chamberlaine, W. H. Pearce, and Yates, in Bengal; and Judson and Boardman in Burmah—but they have sent out to India more than any other portion of the Christian church." After having said, that "of one hundred and twenty-nine European and American missionaries, no less than eighty-four are Baptists," he adds—"Had all the branches of Christ's church done as much for Bengal in proportion to their numbers and wealth, as the Baptists have done, we should have hundreds of missionaries where we have tens."

In a recent volume upon the gospel in Burmah, in which is recited the story of its introduction and marvelous progress among the Burmese and Karens, the wife of the author just quoted, though herself, like her husband, of a different Christian communion, bears yet higher testimony to the Baptists. An English Presbyterian, speaking of that wondrous "story" which Mrs. Wylie so well tells, lately said, as is stated in a recent notice of her work, that "the history of American Baptist missions among the Burmese and Karens, reads like *a continuation of the Acts of the Apostles.*"

An essential part of the missionary work is the translation and circulation of the Holy Scriptures. In this department of evangelical effort, the Baptists have always been distinguished. They have outstripped all others. Even in the time of their sorest persecution, and deepest depression, the Waldensian Baptists were indefatigable in their labors for the diffusion of the pure word of God, not only in their own, but in other communities. Their great leader, Waldo, "caused the Scriptures to be translated into the language of the people, and sent his disciples abroad at the same time, traveling incessantly from one region to another. In his Historical Inquiry, Ten Cate ascribes in great degree to "the circulation of translations of the Bible" the astonishing prevalence of their principles, throughout Europe, before and at the time of the Reformation. "Since the word of God was the foundation upon which they stood, they were desirous that it should be as widely known as possible. The Scriptures could go where the Waldensian preachers could not; and where their preachers had been, their preaching could be confirmed by the Bible." Their "persecutors themselves declared that the translations of the Scriptures must be considered as the chief cause of the spread of the Waldensian opinions," and "with all their might" opposed them. But the Waldenses were not terrified. In the face of all opposition, these noble witnesses for the truth persisted heroically in their blessed work. "When they came into the Netherlands, they took care to translate the Bible into the Dutch and Flemish languages."

The successors of these men, whose descendants were afterward known in Holland as Baptists, inherited their principles and their spirit. Long and patiently did they labor, by the slow process of writing to multiply copies of the Holy Book for those who were perishing for lack of knowledge. At length the art of printing, denounced by the slaves of superstition as the device of the devil, came, a glorious gift from God, to facilitate and lighten their labors. And "before the end of the fifteenth century, more than one Dutch translation of the Scriptures was given to the public; in 1477, at Delft; in 1479, at Gonda; in 1481, at Utrecht; in 1486, at Harlem; in 1487, at Zrolle; and in 1493, at Deventer."

Inspired by Baptist principles, Wickliffe, "morning star of the Reformation," and Tyndale, in England, its very "dawn," have both laid the world under obligations for their translations of the Scriptures, and the self-sacrificing efforts which they made to give them to the people.

Nor have the later Baptists proven recreant to the Bible-loving spirit of their ancestors. The London Quarterly Review, referring, in 1809, to the labors of Carey and his associates, in India, says: "They have translated the whole Bible into Bengali, and have by this time printed it. They are printing the New Testament in the Sanscrit, the Orissa, Mahratta, Hindostani, and Guzarat, and translating it into Persic, Felinga, Karnata, Chinese, the language of the Seikhs and of the Burmans; and in four of these languages they are going on with the whole Bible." After remarking further upon the "extraordinary" character of their achievements, that celebrated journal affirms that "in fourteen years" they "have done more towards spreading the knowledge of the Scriptures among the heathen, than has been accomplished by *all the world besides.*"

In addition to their achievements in translating and publishing the Word of God, "the missionaries of the English Baptist Society, among their *incidental* labors, have written and published fourteen grammars and nine dictionaries, mostly of languages in which no such works previously existed."

In connection with the work of Bible translation by the Baptists, we might say as much of Judson as we have said of Carey. But it is not necessary. All know the achievements, in this behalf, of "Burmah's great Missionary."

In view of all the facts which have been adduced, who shall say that the influence of the Baptists upon the world, has been, is, or is destined to be, slight? Great, however silent and unobserved, has been that influence in all the Christian ages gone by. Great, at this moment, is it in every quarter of the world. And greater, far greater, is it yet to be upon coming generations. "One or two great ideas," says Professor Curtis, "are evidently at work among the masses of thinking men. One is what may be termed *the essential voluntariness of all true religion, and, therefore, of all true church-membership.* That piety is not a thing of mere education, to be learned by rote simply through creed and catechism; not a thing to be professed by proxy, or indeed to be professed at all without the surrender of a man's own heart to God; and that all forms and rites without that are worthless. It is evident, on a moment's reflection, that either this idea must destroy Pedobaptism, or else Pedobaptism must destroy it. Which does the pious Christian wish to be victorious? Certain as destiny it is, that the aggressive principle will here prove triumphant. There is another great truth at work with progressive power, throughout the whole world, both in Church and State. It is *the principle of self-government,* as the most proper of all authorities, because resting with greatest faith and most immediately upon the universal government of God. To that all the revolutions of Europe are tending; to that, the peaceful extension of our own national principles. It were as useless to attempt to silence the thunder by a word, or to roll back the falling waters of Niagara, as to stay the progress of these opinions. The world is full of them, and the churches are full of them. We believe that whoever examines carefully, will perceive that our principles, as Baptists, present the most complete living embodiment of these ideas."[1]

Thus, wide-spread and mighty, under the smiles of Heaven, has been and is the influence of the Baptists in the world. Thus onward has been the course of their principles, despite every difficulty and every foe. And whatever checks, in the Providence of God, may hereafter impede their progress, whatever outward reverses they may suffer, those principles, because they are the principles of Christianity itself, must and will advance until their great mission is fulfilled, and throughout the whole earth "one Lord, one faith, and one baptism" are loyally and lovingly acknowledged.

[1] Communion, pp. 275, 276.

IX.

CONCLUDING REMARKS.

Recapitulation—Nothing Arrogant—No intentional Disparagement of Others—Boastful and Vain-glorious Spirit Disclaimed—The Work commended to the Blessing of God and to the kind and candid Attention of the Reader.

THUS have we seen the apostolic origin and character of the Baptists—their existence in all ages—the scriptural breadth of their views—the expansiveness and liberality of their spirit—the simplicity, strength, and efficiency of their polity—the importance of their position—the extent and beneficial character of their influence upon the world.

The high claims which we have instituted in behalf of the Baptists, will, to some, seem arrogant. And we grant that they would be so, if unsustained by clear and convincing evidence of their validity. Such evidence we think we have furnished. If we have done so, we do not see how arrogance can be charged either against them, or the most emphatic and unequivocal assertion of them. However that may be, we think we shall at least be acquitted of uncharitableness of spirit and harshness of language in their presentation. We have endeavored to speak the truth; and much more in defense of our injured brethren, than in aggression upon others. And we should deeply regret, if, while zealously striving to vindicate the Baptists from unjust charges, we should seem to be unjust to even their most prejudiced and inveterate opponents.

Exception will, perhaps, be taken to what may seem an implied disparagement of the claims of others But, in asserting our own just claims, whatever they may be, we assume no more than we are ready to accord to others. We are perfectly willing that all should make and maintain, as best they can, such claims as they consider just; and however high, if fairly established, we trust we shall not want the candor and the justice to concede them. We ask, for ourselves, a respectful and candid estimate of the evidence we adduce in support of our claims, and a concession of them only in so far as that evidence, when justly and generously weighed, may properly entitle us to it.

Some will probably charge us with a boastful, vain-glorious spirit. But for ourselves and our brethren, we would earnestly disclaim such a spirit. God forbid that we should be of the number of those who, exalting themselves, shall be abased. Any advantage which we may possess, is such as the truth gives us. And for this we would humbly and gratefully acknowledge ourselves wholly indebted to the sovereign grace of the God of truth. So far from indulging a spirit of self-glorification, we would make the very consideration of the favors conferred upon us, an occasion of humility, remembering that of those to whom much is given, much will be required.

With these views, and in this spirit, we commend the foregoing pages to the blessing of God, trusting that they may bear some humble part in promotion of the divine glory, and be of some service, both to those in whose defense they have been prepared, and to those whose unjust imputations have given occasion to their preparation; leading both parties to the cultivation of a deeper devotion to truth and righteousness, and to the exercise of a broader and more fervent charity.

THE END.

www.ingramcontent.com/pod-product-compliance
Lightning Source LLC
LaVergne TN
LVHW050531100826
845148LV00002B/514

* 9 7 8 1 4 2 5 5 1 9 2 1 6 *